The Serial Killer No One Could Catch

Ana Benson

Published by Trellis Publishing, 2021.

THE SERIAL KILLER NO ONE COULD CATCH

First edition. July 13, 2021.

ISBN: 979-8224789689

Written by Ana Benson.

THE SERIAL KILLER NO ONE COULD CATCH

ANA BENSON

ROBERT J GROSS

Serial killers are often caught in a span of five years because they cannot evade the justice forever. But one man managed to ruin many lives over four decades. A suspect in three murders, Robert J Gross was on a police radar many times, but they simply couldn't find any physical evidence connecting him to the crimes. The DNA technology was non-existent back then, and the forensic teams worked with what they had available. But he simply couldn't always be one step ahead of everyone and Robert J Gross had to slip up eventually.

Early life and first signs of trouble

Born in 1952 in Kansas City, Missouri Robert J Gross grew up in a very strict family that valued discipline above anything else. His mother was a social worker while his father worked in a post office. Both of them had a military background and expected their son to behave properly. As a matter of fact, Mrs. Gross was the main disciplinarian, and she didn't hesitate to use physical force on the young Robert. This made the young boy both afraid and mad at his mother who was supposed to be a caring parent. Therefore, Robert did everything he could to make his mother angry. However, the first warning signs that something could be wrong with the boy appeared quite early in his life.

Robert was only eight years old in 1960 when he assaulted a girl who lived in his neighborhood. The full story behind this attack is still unknown, but the investigators did discover that Robert burned a hole in the girl's underwear while she was wearing it. Scared out of her mind, the girl went straight to her parents who contacted Mr. and Mrs. Gross. Appalled by what their son had done, the two of them became even more strict towards Robert. Unfortunately, this incident was just the beginning for the young Robert Gross. He wanted to make his parents angry but also had uncontrollable urges that would come out once he got into his teens.

The incident with the underwear was reported to the authorities, but they didn't even talk to Robert. However, he will be arrested five years later in 1965. Robert burglarized a home and was found by the owners in their bathroom. The scene was horrific because they caught Robert pleasing himself while wearing female underwear he picked up as he rummaged the house. Since Robert was a minor, he was released from the custody. Of course, this didn't mean he was capable of suppressing his urges. Robert once again broke into another house. It was 1967, and he selected a place owned by a young mother. It is very likely that Robert chooses this house because it was in his own neighborhood and not far away from his childhood home. The terrorized woman often spent time alone with her newborn since the husband was always working out of the state.

But the husband was with her on the night that Robert Gross broke into their home for the first time. They were sleeping in the bedroom when they heard strange noises around the house. As the weeks went by, the young mother noticed that the things were moving around the place and she found it very strange. She immediately suspected Gross since he was "the weird kid" who lived down the street but her suspicions were not enough to contact the police. Gross will be caught quickly. While her husband was out of the city, the young mother took her baby to visit one of her friends. A neighbor who lived next door knew that the family was not in the house when they noticed that the lights were turned on. They called the police suspecting that someone was burglarizing the place. What the authorities found was quite shocking for them. Gross was once again caught in the bathroom, wearing a full set of female underwear. The police didn't ask him to change, and they led him out of the house dressed like that.

Robert's parents were called to the police station, and they begged the authorities not to punish their teenage son. Mr. and Mrs. Gross promised that they would stop his erratic behavior, confirming that this will be the last time their son was found in a similar situation. The Gross family was religious and had a good reputation in the area, so the police didn't want to press any charges against a tall and lanky teen who was probably going through some sort of a phase. Unfortunately, this incident left a lasting mark on the young mother who was the victim after all. Robert's parents did come to talk to her once he was released from the custody, assuring her that he will stay away from her home. But the unnamed woman was still tormented by everything she went through during that time period, and it left her feeling uncomfortable. She thought about pressing charges against the teenager but was assured by a local psychologist that it is not uncommon for boys of that age to explore their sexuality and it will probably never happen again.

Robert Gross did indeed continue to go to high school regularly. He was a good student who was very involved in school sports. His tall stature allowed him to be a part of the football team and he was a great player. As far as the police know, Robert didn't get into any more troubles as a teenager. Once he graduated, Gross enrolled in Missouri University of Science and Technology in Rolla. He majored in engineering. But things didn't go as well as he had expected in the university, so he dropped out after finishing the first semester. Gross moved back to Kansas City and found a job as a sheet metal worker. He didn't want to live with his parents and craved independence he tasted at the university, so he rented his own place. This also gave him the freedom to do whatever he wanted.

The history of abusing women

Gross was quite good looking and women seemed attracted to him. One of them was Janet Manuel who started dating Robert Gross in 1973. She was a nurse and though that Gross treated her well in the beginning. He even introduced her to his parents which Janet found endearing. However, she also noticed that his mother was a bit controlling. Janet Manuel trusted Gross, so she allowed him to take nude photos of her which was a huge mistake. He soon began acting oddly, forbidding Janet to go out with her friends, accusing her of cheating on him, and regularly beating her if she didn't comply with his wishes. One evening he saw her dancing with another man and proceeded to show images of naked Janet to her friends. She was very hurt and they started fighting. Janet managed to get to her car, but it was clearly broken since it couldn't go at its normal speed. Scared for her life, Janet drove to her parents and found Gross sitting with them with her nude photos in his hands.

Gross told Janet's parents that she was cheating on him and accused their daughter of other horrible things. When he left the house enraged, Janet called the police, but they couldn't do a thing about it back in the day. Gross couldn't let go so he called Janet's house repeatedly, often very late at night. He was seen parked in front of the home as well which scared Janet a lot. She was sure that he would try to physically harm her. In the following months, Gross managed to sabotage Janet's car and slash her tires. But after seven months of torture, everything stopped and Gross moved on. He did have steady girlfriends, but that didn't stop him from hiring sex workers. He was quite known for that in the area and sex workers avoided him because he was abusive most of the time. Gross also developed a fascination with the firearm and started collecting as many guns as rifles as possible, making him a very dangerous individual to be around of.

The first murders

He also developed an obsession with massage parlors, particularly the V.I.P. Health Studio which was located in an undeveloped part of Kansas City. The girls who worked there didn't like Gross and often stayed away from him every time he entered the parlor. But one worker from the V.I.P. Health Studio saw Gross as someone who could help her get away from her bad marriage. Her name was Wanda Conkling and she started dating Gross in 1976. She had two boys from a marriage to William Cadwalader, and the two of them were separated at the time because Cadwalader was abusive. Gross took care of Wanda Conkling, protecting her from her ex-husband who would drop by her house occasionally to either abuse her physically or verbally. But when Wanda's friend Kathy Zeysing heard about her relationship with Gross, she connected the dots, figuring out that Gross was a teenager who broke into her sister's home years ago. Kathy told this detail to Wanda, warning her friend that he as well could be dangerous.

Wanda reconciled with her former husband in 1979, and the two of them decided to try to make things work for the sake of their two boys. She severed all contact to Gross, but he was not ready to let go. As a matter of fact, Gross spent weeks wallowing around, complaining to strangers in bars. One of his friends recalled that he said the following: *"She made me love her and then she did this to me."* As in previous failed relationships he had, Gross continued to call Wanda's house repeatedly. Luckily, she lived alone so she usually answered the phone herself, but she was afraid that her husband might one day pick up the receiver and discover that it was Gross on the other end of the line. Gross didn't stop there, of course. He had other scare tactics he used on Wanda as well. He would drove to her house in the middle of the night, park in her driveway and put on the lights in his car, illuminating the entire home. Once Wanda got up, he would speed away, leaving the woman terrified.

Wanda spoke to her friends about the things Gross was doing to her and that she was afraid things will not end up well. On the other hand, she managed to reconnect with her ex-husband, and the two of them mended the relationship. They decided to book a trip to California at the beginning of February and go on a second honeymoon. Meanwhile, one of Wanda's friends from the massage parlor told Gross he should stop contacting Wanda for good and that she was going away on a mini holiday with her ex-husband. This enraged Gross who jumped off his chair and stormed out of the room screaming that he was going to talk to Wanda. This all happened on February 5th, 1979, one day before the trip.

Wanda didn't answer the phone the next week but her friends didn't think something serious was going on since she did say that she will be out of town. However, the mailman grew suspicious since he noticed that the front door of Wanda's house was ajar for a couple of days and nobody has been picking up the mail. Not to forget that he couldn't see or hear Wanda's dog who would greet him every time he was in the yard. The mailman spoke to Wanda's next door neighbor and he confirmed that something weird might have happened. Concerned, the neighbor called the police who arrived at the given address and entered the house. Inside they discovered two dead bodies laying on the floor. They were identified as Wanda and William. The wounds on their bodies were brutal and it was confirmed they were shot with a shotgun. Wanda's dead body was almost unrecognizable since she was shot in the head.

After examining the crime scene, the detectives concluded that the killer entered the house through the front door, probably by kicking it down. Since the suitcases were in the middle of the living room, it was obvious that Wanda and William were packing for their trip when they were gunned down. Just like any US city back in the 1970s, Kansas City had a higher murder rate than the average. But the law enforcement quickly put together a group of twelve investigators who were supposed to be working on this case. Unfortunately, they didn't have any physical evidence that could point to a single killer, so the investigators needed to take a closer look at the people in Wanda's and William's lives. Not to forget that doing ballistic testing on the remains of the shotgun bullet was near impossible and connecting it to a weapon was difficult.

The investigators quickly uncovered the information about William's past and his connections to the local mafia. He was a thief and the chances were he was the main target. The Kansas City mafia was known for their brutal killings and they didn't hesitate to eliminate anyone who tried to cross them. On the other hand, Wanda's friends mentioned Robert Gross to the investigators, and once they started examining him thoroughly, it was clear that he should have been their number one suspect from the very beginning. Unfortunately, the team of the investigators already blew their budget and were unable to continue the investigation. But they did conclude that Gross fit the profile of the killer considering his history of violence towards the women, his vast gun collection, and the fact that he hated his mother. Also, he didn't have an alibi for the entire week when Wanda and William were murdered. Unfortunately, Gross managed to slip away from the police because they simply didn't have any physical evidence placing him on the scene. The accusations and hear-say were not enough for the investigators to pursue him.

The disappearance of Cheryl Morris

Cheryl Morris was an incredibly bubbly and easy-going young woman who always pushed the boundaries. With her positive attitude, she was an embodiment of the hippie culture of the time. She grew up on a farm but quickly discovered rock n roll and even played bass guitar in a band. She spent her twenties traveling around but made a decision to enroll in a university and earn a degree when she turned thirty. She moved to Kansas City after getting accepted to Longview Community College. Unfortunately, she could only afford to go there part-time and worked as a waitress in a Mexican restaurant. Robert Gross frequented that same restaurant ever since he was a teenager because his mother worked there and he enjoyed the food they were making. This is where he met Cheryl Morris and he became infatuated with her.

Gross was quite stubborn and he invited Cheryl out a couple of times. She continued to reject his advances which made him hurt. Cheryl didn't like his vibe and thought that he simply wanted to sleep with her. Just like before, he began harassing her. First, he started calling her on the phone both at home and at work. That escalated into fully blown stalking that included slashed tires on Cheryl's car. She talked openly about how creepy Gross was to her friends and co-workers. Cheryl's cousin Patrick Cook said the following about the incidents: *"He wouldn't take no for an answer. She was scared of him."*

Cheryl Morris left the Mexican restaurant on November 4th, 1981 around 09:30 PM. She had just finished her shift and planned to drop by her friend's place because the two of them needed to study for the upcoming exams. It was the last time anyone saw the young woman alive. Her family became concerned after two days because they didn't hear back from Cheryl. She had a habit of phoning them regularly and talking about what she was doing. Her parents called the Kansas City Police Department who began the search for Cheryl right away. The investigators retraced her steps on the night of her disappearance and discovered her car parked near her friend's house. However, the friend she planned to study with told the detectives Cheryl never arrived at her place. Cheryl's colleagues from the restaurant rallied together and started searching for her in the surrounding woods, hoping to find any clue to what happened to their friend. They were unsuccessful.

Gross entered the investigation when Cheryl's mother mentioned that she was constantly harassed by him. This alarmed the police officers because they knew that stalkers could get violent easily. However, a couple of investigators did remember reading his name in one of the old cold cases as a possible suspect. They dug further and found out that he was investigated in the death of Wanda Conkling and William Cadwalader. The police went to his house in order to talk to Gross, but he was standoffish from the very beginning, claiming that he did see Morris in the Mexican restaurant but he had never invited her out.

The detectives didn't believe a word he said because they had the previous report and it was obvious that Gross used the same modus operandi on all of his female victims. The police were determined to catch him this time so they organized several teams who followed

Gross wherever he went, hoping he might lead them to Cheryl or perhaps make a mistake that could indicate where the girl is. But Gross was always one step ahead of them, mostly because he was aware of the police officers who monitored him. He knew how to lose them in the traffic, and they had problems keeping up with Gross. The police needed to have a body or any type of trace in order to put Gross behind the bars. But they couldn't uncover a single thing. So the entire case went cold which made Cheryl's family fall into despair. They were certain Gross was behind this crime but there was no way to prove it.

They dug deeper into Richard Gross' past and uncovered he had a long history of violence towards the women, including a reported attack on a sex worker in 1977. He picked up a woman, and once they got to his house, he forced her to do things she didn't agree to do in the first place. When she tried to get away, he attacked her with a tire iron.

The stalking of Dana Rexrode and arson

Dana Rexrode met Robert Gross in February of 1984. Even though she said that he wasn't particularly interesting to her, the two of them started dating. They haven't been together for a very long time when they decided to get away to Colorado for the weekend. Dana woke up in the middle of the night because she had a creepy feeling. She was very right because she saw Gross looking at her naked body. Dana broke things off as soon as they got back to Kansas City but that triggered Gross and he quickly spiraled into his old behavior. He called Dana constantly and hang up the phone. But Dana didn't want to let go so easily, so she persisted when it came to reporting Gross' harassment. He broke into Dana's home, stealing some of her clothes, photos, and a gun. Luckily for her, Robert Gross made a major mistake during this time.

On July 15th, 1984 a house exploded in a quiet neighborhood of Kansas City. The witnesses saw a man running away from fire and jumping into a vehicle. He was clearly burned, so the police simply waited for him to show up in one of the local emergency rooms. It took Gross almost one hour to make a decision to seek help from the doctors for his burns. He refused to say how he got injured but the staff in the emergency room suspected that he might be the arsonist wanted by the police. The police located Gross' car and concluded that it was damaged in the fire as well. They discovered cans with fuel and a hand-drawn map to the burned house. It once belonged to Gross' partner who co-owned a bar with him. Accidentally, the investigators also found a shotgun that could have been used in the unsolved murders in 1979. The authorities had enough evidence to put Robert Gross behind the bars this time.

Hoping they could find proof that would confirm that he was involved in the murders of Wanda Conkling and William Cadwalader, as well as in the disappearance of Cheryl Morris, the Kansas City Police Department got a search warrant for Gross' home. Once they got in, they did find Wanda's ring and some handwritten notes connected to Cheryl Morris. However, they also stumbled upon cocaine and scales used to measure the amount of the drug. Just a couple of hours later, Robert Gross was charged with arson and threatening Dana Rexrode. The trial was scheduled soon, and Gross pleaded not guilty. He was then charged for cocaine possession and stealing firearm in September of 1985. The prosecution mentioned that he was an abusive stalker who probably harmed many women in his life. On the other hand, the defense said that there is no proof for any of those claims. He was found guilty and sentenced to fifteen years behind the bars, as well as $30,000 fine.

The discovery of Cheryl Morris body

It was September 3rd, 1987 when a father and a son were walking around the rural parts of Raymore, Missouri. They passed by a concrete cistern, and the man opened up the cover. He was terrified by what he saw inside. It was a decomposing body of a woman. The forensic experts got to the scene immediately and concluded that she was strangled. She was identified as Cheryl Morris who was missing since the beginning of the decade. Her family was devastated by the discovery, but it brought them closure. They were now certain that Robert Gross was behind this crime. Cass County Sheriff Department took over the case, and it became active once again. Unfortunately, the investigation led nowhere and they had no evidence that could prove that Gross was the murderer.

The parole and the missed opportunities

Robert Gross was up for a parole in February of 1992 after serving a little bit over half of his sentence. He was the exemplary prisoner who behaved well during the time he was locked up. The parole board was informed about the fact that he was a prime suspect in three murders but once again, the claims needed to be backed up by physical evidence. Robert Gross was paroled in 1994, and Cass County Sherriff Department managed to file a charge against him as soon as he was released. They did find an eye-witness claiming that they saw a car which resembled Gross' during the late winter of 1981. However, Gross' attorney managed to drop the charges easily. Robert Gross was a free man. He stayed away from trouble until 2002 when he was charged with stalking and got sent back to prison. Gross was released in 2004.

He moved back to his parents' home and did his best to blend in. Deep in his fifties, Gross appeared as a helpful and lovable neighbor. He didn't mention that he was a convicted felon and attended church regularly. The people who lived in the same street liked him even though some of them thought that he might have a mental illness because he sometimes mumbled things to himself.

The return to the massage parlors

Old habits die hard, and that is very clear in the case of Robert Gross. He frequented the massage parlors in the area where he would go to get the standard treatments. The women who worked there didn't like Gross at all because, after some time, he would start acting oddly. He asked one of them to have sex with him, and the woman refused right away. Soon enough, the workers from the massage parlor were harassed by someone who would damage their cars or slash the tires. Suspecting that Gross might be behind these deeds, he was banned from all massage parlors in the area. Then, a surveillance camera caught him damaging a vehicle.

He couldn't stand the fact that he was forbidden from these establishments, so Gross stormed into Tea Spa massage parlor one day and got into the back room where he took all of his clothes off. The women who worked that shift told him to get out and that he will not get a massage. Enraged, Gross started breaking things around the parlor, and rubbing his naked body on the woman. He grabbed her breasts as she tried to get away to call for help. A man came into the parlor and took Gross away. The police were contacted immediately and the name Robert Gross was very familiar to them.

The Kansas City Police Department received another call from a massage parlor owner the next day, and the woman told them she saw Gross near her house. The police decided to follow him by using GPS technology and had noticed some unusual movements. That was enough for them to get a warrant to search his house. They discovered a real arsenal of weapons in there, as well as the addresses of the women who worked in the massage parlors. Sensing that the man is a real threat, the police arrested him. He is now in prison, waiting for the trial which will begin in January of 2019. He has been charged with possession of a firearm as a felon, as well as with a sexual assault. There are no murder charges but hopefully, this dangerous man who evaded the authorities for decades will be jailed for good this time.

HUSBAND KILLER DONNA YAKLICH

JESSI DIXON

Old-fashioned police work

In December 1985, a narcotics detective was shot and killed in the driveway of his farm in Pueblo, Colorado, where he lived with his five children and his wife, Donna Yaklich. Initially, authorities suspected Dennis' death was linked to his work in law enforcement, but a tip led them to two teenage shooters – and eventually, back to Dennis' wife, Donna.

However, attorneys for Donna Yaklich argued that Dennis had been beating his wife. The murder, they claimed, was a battered woman's desperate attempt to escape a lifetime of abuse – or potentially becoming a murder victim herself, like Dennis' first wife, who is thought to have died of a diet drug overdose in 1977.

Yaklich was finally acquitted of first-degree murder after a mistrial and a second trial that has been described as "grueling," but was convicted on the charge of conspiracy for hiring gunmen to kill her husband. Her sentence was forty years in prison, but was released to a halfway house in 2005, after serving close to eighteen years.

The young men Yaklich had hired to carry out the murder were also arrested and sentenced. Charles Greenwell, who was only 16 when the crime was committed, received a sentence of twenty years while his brother Eddie, who had been 25, received thirty years.

However, while Yaklich's claims of abuse weren't enough to get her off on the premise of self-defence, they did encourage authorities to reopen their investigation into the death of Barbara Yaklich. According to a cold case team, the investigation was "incomplete."

"This case needed some good, old-fashioned police work," said team lead Steve Johnson, with the Colorado Bureau of Investigation. "In my opinion, I have seen better documented traffic accidents."

Discrepancies were found in the autopsy report, which originally claimed Barbara had fainted from taking diet pills. When her body-builder husband, Dennis, tried "energetically" to resuscitate her, she suffered bleeding in her abdomen. However, administering CPR is not an appropriate reaction to fainting – and as a police officer trained in CPR, Dennis would have known this.

Still, there was apparently no examination of the potential crime scene, and when Dennis was asked to take a polygraph to support his defense, he refused.

Denver-area pathologist Michael Doberson determined that the conclusions in the report were "very unusual" – the internal damage Barbara had suffered, he claimed, was more likely caused by a blow to the abdomen. Doberson included his findings in a letter to Johnson dated in 2005, stating that in his opinion, "the entire scenario is simply not credible." A second forensic pathologist concurred with Doberson's conclusions.

According to reports, Barbara's liver tore open and her abdomen was quickly filled with more than 2,000 millilitres of blood – nearly 40 per cent of her total blood volume, and more than twice as much as is typical in a victim of a fatal car accident.

Investigators are now considering her death as "suspicious," with the tear caused by a blunt force trauma consistent with "punches and knee drops to the upper abdomen," according to pathologist Stephen Cina. However, the autopsy report showed no other indications that would reveal a pattern of abuse – no recorded discoloration, bruising, or external signs of beatings.

While the investigation into Barbara's death is now complete, the case hasn't been closed. According to the coroner and the Pueblo County Sheriff, the public deserves answers to the questions that have been raised.

The family man

Donna Yaklich met Dennis and his children only a few months after Barbara's death. According to Yaklich, the plan was to move in with the family for the summer and help him get the kids back into their home, since they were temporarily staying with Dennis' mother.

"I had no expected to fall in love with the children, who so desperately needed someone," Yaklich said. "They were grieving for their mother, so I couldn't bear to leave them."

Barbara had died on Valentine's Day, and had "appeared fine" as her children left for school that morning. However, an hour later, Barbara was dead – and Dennis was the only person who had been with her as she died. According to some reports, there are members of the community who do continue to question Dennis' involvement in the death of his first wife, including at least one of his former co-workers.

"Dennis' fellow officers knew he was out of control, but they also knew when they needed him he would be the first to go through the door," Yaklich said. "No one who worked with him would go against him."

It was this feeling of hopelessness that eventually led Yaklich to hire gunmen to kill her husband, in an effort to finally end the ongoing abuse. She'd moved in with Dennis when she was only 22 and he was 30. The children were aged 3, 9, 11, and 12 – and she immediately fell into the role of step-mother, despite the abuse which began only a month after Yaklich moved in. She said she attempted to leave a few times, but always went back.

"I feared Dennis, but at the same time I felt at home with him because I had grown up in an abusive environment," Yaklich said. "I fell into the trap of thinking if I could make everything perfect for him, he wouldn't get mad at me or at the kids. Dennis' threats to kill me or kill someone I loved if I ever left again kept me there."

Dennis even threatened to use his access to federal law enforcement agents against Yaklich, telling her that she'd never be able to get away from him – these agents were capable of fiding anyone, anywhere. Eventually, she said, "I lost myself. I lost hope."

"I became very depressed and mad at myself because I had no trusted my instincts about leaving the relationship when the abuse started," Yaklich said. "Suicidal thoughts became an answer. Then came homicidal thoughts."

Looking back, Yaklich admitted that she wished she had listened to those first instincts, but eventually came to a point where she no longer cared. However, she said she has been working on bettering herself since being convicted and sentenced.

"Being in prison is similar to the prison I put myself in while I was married to Dennis," she said. "However, prison is also what you make of it, so I've enrolled in educational programs, had therapy, and also taken care of myself. Things I should have done in society."

A professional abuser

At a menacing 6'5" and 280 pounds, Dennis Yaklich was a competitive weightlifter who continuously used steroids to supplement his workouts – despite the fact that they also enhanced his aggressive tendencies. While the officers who worked with him conceded that he was always the go-to guy for breaking down a door or clearing a room, he was difficult to manage. In fact, when he did become confrontational, even a supervisor threatened to shoot him because they had no other way to defend themselves.

A former partner once stated that he felt he always had to "clean up after Dennis," and other co-workers have admitted they "dreaded" working with Dennis, because of his aggressive and unpredictable behaviour. Some of his closest colleagues have even confessed that Dennis displayed some "abusive tactics" on the job – while denying the complaints of citizens against him.

Yaklich endured what can only be described as domestic terrorism. While the physical abuse, which included slapping, choking, kicking, and pushing her down stairs as well as sadistic sexual assaults, was indeed disabling and troubling, the psychological abuse was almost worse. According to Yaklich, the threat of death loomed constantly – Dennis would put his gun to her head and threaten to kill her, point his finger at her in the shape of a gun and blow on it after miming shooting her with it, and even beating her under the cover of darkness so she wouldn't be able to prepare for the blows.

The physical abuse has been corroborated by a number of independent witnesses, including a mailman who reported seeing bruises on Yaklich's face, and a telephone repairman who had been called in twice to fix phones after Dennis had yanked them out of the wall in a fit of rage.

Following Yaklich's arrest, the repairman spoke with detectives investigating Dennis' death and said the bruises he had seen on Yaklich's neck and cheek were so prominent, he noticed them "at a glance." The detective inquired how the repairman could recall the incident so vividly, and he admitted that in his line of work, he sees "a lot of things like that in the low income areas and the projects, but I was shocked to see a cop's wife all bruised up like she was."

Cries unheard

Yaklich's first documented attempt for police intervention came in 1982, when she called Dennis' partner to explain that Dennis was "out of control" and threatening to kill her. The detective advised her to leave right away, but she said she was too afraid – if she left, she said, Dennis had told her he would kill her entire family, starting with her father.

Believing that Yaklich was in fear for her life, the detective immediately went to inform his supervisor about the call he'd received about his partner. According to the detective, the supervisor had gestured to indicate that he should just forget the call – it was none of their business – and the incident went unreported.

It was then that Yaklich realized that trying to get help from the police would be completely futile, and she would need to seek support elsewhere.

The next year, in November of 1983, Yaklich endured a short and traumatic visit with a psychologist. After Yaklich "sobbed uncontrollably" through the entire session, the psychologist recommended she leave her husband – but failed to offer her suggestions to muster the courage needed to do so, or what steps she could take to do it safely.

Since Yaklich was required to provide her abusive husband with detailed accounts of where she spent all her time, there was no way for her to continue therapy with regular appointments. She never went back for another session.

A few months later, Yaklich escaped to a battered women's shelter in Denver, in February of 1984. Dennis pleaded with her to come home, and even went so far as to promise that he would try to change – and because she was ashamed to go back to him again, Yaklich told the counselors that she was leaving the state.

Still, the abuse hadn't stopped another year later. Early in 1985, Yaklich tried talking to friends and family members – telling them she needed advice because Dennis was going to kill her. These claims were shrugged off by everyone she turned to, and the abuse began to escalate.

Feeling as though she had no other options, Yaklich began looking for an opportunity to kill herself. Her attempts failed, however, when she realized she would be abandoning her young son and step-children with their abusive father – and after witnessing the struggles of Barbara's children as they grieved the loss of their mother, she was unable to force that situation on her own child.

Later that year, the Pueblo Sheriff's Department received a 911 call from Yaklich's mother. One of the step-children had called Yaklich's parents after hearing what they thought was Dennis pushing Yaklich through a plate glass window. While it turned out that the noise was caused by just a bowl hitting the floor, the officers who responded barely acknowledged Yaklich.

In fact, their inspection of the situation involved a brief conversation with Dennis followed by a tour of the gym Dennis was building on the property. The situation only reinforced Yaklich's desperate situation on the other side of the blue line – living in fear of an abusive spouse with no support or protection from the authorities.

Finally, on December 12, 1985, one of Yaklich's friends finally responded to her pleas for help. A neighbour, Eddie Greenwell, waited at the Yaklich family's farm with his younger brother, Charles, into the early morning hours. When Dennis returned home after working a night shift, the brothers shot and killed him. Yaklich was inside the house, sleeping.

According to court documents, Yaklich had "approached several people" in an attempt to have her husband killed, and had met with Eddie Greenwell many times over a period of eight months. The Greenwell brothers were paid $4,200 in installments after the murder was committed – although the brothers testified they had been promised $45,000.

The story of the tragic marriage was detailed in a made-for-television movie called *Cries Unheard: The Donna Yaklich Story*. The film was released in 1994 and starred former Charlie's Angel Jaclyn Smith as Yaklich.

A disturbing conflict of interest

After Dennis was killed, the Pueblo Police Department – Dennis' employer – carried out an investigation into his death, despite the fact that the murder actually took place in the jurisdiction of the Pueblo Sheriff's Office. Lead roles in the inquiry were awarded to narcotics detectives – Dennis' partners.

The District Attorney was also a personal friend of Dennis', and even admitted to being a material witness in his own case. At the time of the trial, DA Sandstrom was wrapped up in a highly contested election – and this clear political agenda, combined with the attempts of the police department to hide its role in Yaklich's abuse and ultimately, Dennis' death, indicate incredible prejudice against Yaklich from the very beginning.

Not that Yaklich was surprised. After attempting to secure the help of police several times during the course of her abusive marriage, it was obvious to Yaklich that law enforcement was not on her side.

Still, the jury acquitted Yaklich of the charge of first-degree murder. Several jurors even thought Yaklich deserved to be acquitted of all charges, but felt intimidated by the Pueblo Police Department – and feared potential retaliation. Instead, the jury voted guilty on the charge of conspiracy to commit murder, believing that the fair-minded judge would give the battered wife the minimum sentence of eight years.

The probation supervisor who had conducted Yaklich's pre-sentencing investigation testified that Yaklich would be an "excellent candidate" for sentencing alternatives outside of the Department of Corrections, and gave the court his recommendation for the minimum sentence. His testimony affirmed the sense of desperation Yaklich claimed to be struggling with.

"I really felt that whether they did what she wanted done, to have Dennis killed, or whether Dennis found out and killed her, it didn't matter," he said. "She was at a point in her life where either was satisfactory."

However, the late Judge Seavy who presided over the trial chose to overlook the circumstances leading to Dennis' murder and remanded Yaklich to the Department of Corrections for a sentence of forty years. According to the judge, Yaklich "started this whole scenario," and therefore deserved to serve a period of time "in excess of the longest Greenwell's sentence."

"We cannot overlook the fact that Yaklich's participation in the death of her husband was not merely peripheral," stated court documents. "Had it not been for Yaklich, the Greenwells would not have been involved in this murder. Thus, in our view, we would be establishing poor public policy if Yaklich were to escape punishment by virtue of an unprecedented application of self-defense while the Greenwells were convicted of murder."

Still, the jurors were shocked and horrified by the severity of Judge Seavy's harsh sentence. More than half of the serving jurors submitted letters expressing their disappointment with the resulting sentence to a judge who presided over Yaklich's sentencing reconsideration a few years later. These letters were dismissed by that judge, however, who felt "that they must not allow for personal sympathy to influence their decision." Several of the jurors who served on the initial trial event went on to diligently advocate for Yaklich's early release, eighteen years later.

According to Dr. Lenore Walker, who counseled and evaluated Yaklich and provided expert testimony at her trial, Judge Seavy was "using the court and a woman's life to express his own ignorance of a battered woman's plight."

The conspiracy

According to court documents, Yaklich did receive payments totalling more than $250,000 under her late husband's three life insurance policies – leading to a theory that the motivation that pushed her to arrange her husband's death was to obtain this insurance money. The defense argued that Yaklich suffered from "battered woman syndrome," and that the conspiracy to commit murder was a "justifiable act of self-defence ... committed under duress resulting from years of physical and psychological battering by her husband."

"Yaklich lived in a constant state of fear of her husband," the defense argued. "At the time of his death, she believed she was in imminent danger of being killed by him or receiving great bodily injury from him."

The defense went on to explain that many battered women are unable to safely leave their abusive spouses – and in fact, the abuse often escalates as a result of a separation. Abusers have also been known to pursue their victims after they've left, subjecting them to "brutal attacks."

"Additionally, battered women may not psychologically or emotionally have the alternative of leaving the abuser because of their low self-esteem, their emotional and economic dependency, the absence of another place to go, and the woman's legitimate fear of the abuser's response to her leaving," stated the defense. "Battered women become trapped in their own fear and often feel that their only recourse is to kill the batterer or be killed."

Several people involved with the case, including District Attorney Sandstrom, have stated that if Yaklich had gone ahead and committed the murder herself, "she would have walked." However, the DA and many others also question the validity of Yaklich's testimony, including that Dennis was abusing her – maintaining the theory that Yaklich conspired to have him killed just to receive the insurance money.

The DA even stated that "if she had shot him herself, there would be no issue" – leading some to wonder if Sandstrom sees money as an acceptable motive for murder, as long as you follow through with it on your own.

Like most battered women, Yaklich both loved and hated her husband. Killing him herself would have been difficult, as she was afraid that as soon as she pointed a gun at him to save herself and her children, the love she had for him would "override her fear of him," and cause her to second-guess her decision. The ramifications from that could have bene deadly.

Another concern for Yaklich was her husband's established persona of invincibility – one he had carefully instilled in her over years of repeated psychological and physical abuse. Not only did Yaklich struggle to trust in her own ability to kill her husband, she struggled to believe that he would ever really die.

One of the prosecution's expert witnesses, Dr. Alice Brill, said in her testimony that Yaklich didn't meet the traditional profile of a battered woman. These women, according to Brill, generally kill their spouses with little premeditation and show little interest in pursuing relationships with other men – while Yaklich spent at least ten months planning her husband's murder, and had had at least one extramarital affair about a year before Dennis was killed.

Dennis' children also continue to question Yaklich's testimony, stating that none of them had ever witnessed any physical abuse from Dennis during the eight years of the couple's marriage. After Yaklich's parole hearing in October 2005, Dennis' daughter Vanessa fought back tears while talking about the court's decision to release Yaklich after she'd only served eighteen years of her forty-year sentence.

"It's devastating – I don't believe justice has prevailed," she said. "My father died at age 38. He was stripped of his opportunity to live life. He was prevented from raising his children, from seeing us grow up and accomplishing our goals."

Vanessa stated that Yaklich's claims of beatings and abuse were "an outright lie" – and that the depiction of the family's life shown in the TV-movie *Cries Unheard* were based entirely on prison interviews with Yaklich herself, with no supporting evidence or facts contributed by other relatives or friends.

Vanessa added that just two months before her father was killed, Yaklich had told her that Dennis had asked for a divorce – but that the couple planned to delay the proceedings until after the Christmas holidays, for the sake of the younger children. This story has been corroborated by Dennis' brother, who said Dennis told him over the phone that he planned to divorce Yaklich once the holidays had passed.

"(Dennis') life was taken because he was going to divorce my step-mother and not because she was the victim of abuse," Vanessa said. "I never feared my father, nor did I observe any abuse, whether it be psychological or physical, perpetrated by him. His demeanor was calm and loving, his words encouraging and supportive. I can honestly state my step-mother did not provide my siblings or myself with the same."

According to Vanessa, Yaklich didn't show any grief or remorse after Dennis had been killed – and even slapped Vanessa when she began to cry at her father's funeral. She went on to detail the ongoing "injustice," claiming to defend her father since he is no longer able to defend himself.

"My stepmother's legal defense was paid for by my father's life insurance proceeds and my family and I believe she profited from the made-for-television monstrosity," Vanessa said. "Most recently, her financial status has provided her with the ability to hire a media publicist."

Questions also remain about the relationship Yaklich had with her defense attorney, John Giduck. Records show Giduck and Yaklich took a romantic vacation to Jamaica together prior to her arrest in March 1986 – a getaway funded entirely from the death benefit Yaklich received after having her husband murdered.

In fact, the vacation was cut short when Yaklich was notified of the charges that were being brought against her, and surrendered to police upon her return to Pueblo. Most of the insurance money had already been spent by the time Yaklich was arrested.

According to information reported in the Colorado Springs Gazette, Yaklich had been involved in an extramarital affair about a year before Dennis' murder, and had begun a romantic relationship with Giduck only weeks after her husband's death. Giduck had apparently attended Dennis' funeral, where he had given Yaklich his business card and told him to call if she needed anything.

Yaklich reached out to him a few days later, after police asked her to verify the statement she'd given with a routine polygraph test.

A safe and abuse-free life

Still, Yaklich had a spotless record prior to her incarceration, which continued even after she was sent to prison – a testament to her strength of character. According to prison records, Yaklich managed to vigilantly avoid conflict and strictly followed the many rules surrounding prison life. Despite being forced into an environment filled with trouble, Yaklich managed to stay out of it through her entire eighteen-year term.

During her incarceration, Yaklich obtained an associate's degree as well as a Bachelor's degree in psychology – while working in maintenance and then in a computer-refurbishing program at the correctional facility. According to staff there, Yaklich was a hard and industrious worker, even volunteering her time as a member of the Fire Response Team, comprised of prisoners trained in firefighting and first aid.

Yaklich has also volunteered with several programs that support victims of abuse, earning high praise from her Department of Corrections supervisors regarding the effectiveness of her work with young people. She encourages victims of domestic abuse to seek support from therapy groups to find the strength to break away from an abusive partner – to learn how to stay away emotionally and physically.

"Educating ourselves about the issues and statistics relative to domestic violence will help us pass this information on to the next generation," Yaklich said. "Our children need to learn that they have the right to safe and abuse-free lives."

SO DAMN EVIL

GERALDINE PAGE

Louise Melanie "Louise" May was looking for a place to stay.

She had three children but had them taken away as the courts declared her to be an unfit parent because of her drug addiction. At the age of 23, she needed to get her life back together.

Things seemingly could not get any worse for the recovering addict.

But then she arrived at the home of Kerry Dalton seeking help.

"I don't have anywhere to go," Louise said, realizing that her audience in Kerry Lyn Dalton was only half paying attention. "Rob is in jail. They took away my kids. Damn CPS."

The frazzled haired twenty-eight-year-old alternated between staring at the television and smoking on the meth pipe. She took a deep toke on the pipe and let the smoke out.

"You can stay with me," she finally said.

"Oh my God, thank you," Louise said.

"But it is only until Rob gets out," Kerry said.

"I understand. I understand. No problem."

But Louise had a problem. Meth addiction.

Now she had added another problem in Kerry Lyn Dalton.

"Kerry was a queen in the subculture of meth and alcoholism if there is such a thing," forensic psychologist Greta Smith said. "She had been married twice and had five children by three different men. It was amazing how Kerry Dalton even survived to the age of 28. Unemployable, she was the epitome of a bully and would do anything to get her way. She had little regard for the rights or feelings of other people, running roughshod over everyone in her path."

Unfortunately for Louise, she had gotten in Kerry's way.

Kerry would be arrested for drug possession and hauled off to jail for a short stint. She had been Louise's supplier and Louise needed her fix.

But she had no money.

So she began pawning off things she found around the house during a spur of the moment "garage sales." Some of Kerry's old jewelry would be sold off in exchange for drugs.

But when Kerry was released from prison and found out that her stuff had been pawned off, she became more than livid.

She became homicidal.

"Kerry took the theft as a personal affront," Smith said. "This was a fragile living situation between two drug addicts. Junkies. They had little regard for one another and really see each other as utilities to use or supply drugs. Louise is willing to sell out Kerry's stuff while Kerry is willing to kill Louise to gain revenge."

On June 26th, 1988, Kerry confronted Louise at the mobile home. Three other people in their drug dealing clique soon arrived, Mark Lee Tompkins, Sheryl Baker and another transient named "George".

Kerry ordered Louise to sit down and tied her to a chair. She then began torturing her, splicing off and electrical cord and burning her with it.

Louise screamed in pain.

Tompkins then began joining in the torture, jabbing at the defenseless Louise with a screwdriver.

The two then demanded that Sheryl partake in the abuse as well. Reluctantly, Sheryl complied.

"Sheryl felt as if they would have killed her if she didn't do as she was told," Smith said.

After the course of a few hours, the three then took turns torturing Louise.

Kerry enjoyed shocking her captive with the electric cord, laughing as Louise screamed. Seeking to raise the stakes, her boyfriend took an iron skillet and smashed it against the back of Louise's head.

"They hit her with such force that it made a dent in the pan," Smith said.

Kerry's sadism was still not satiated. She kept thinking of different ways to torture Louise then came up with the idea to inject her with some battery acid. Her boyfriend got a syringe and they plunged the battery acid into her vein as well as poured it down her throat.

"Kerry was a sadist," Smith said. "She justified her torture of Louise to the fact that the woman sold a few items of her jewelry and got maybe twenty-five bucks for it."

Tompkins then put Louise out of her misery by stabbing her in the neck with the screwdriver. She fell to the ground and he began stomping on her head until she died.

What happened to Louise's body after remains shrouded in mystery and hearsay.

Later that evening, a sheriff arrived at the mobile home on a burglary call. He saw no evidence of a burglary but did describe one of the residents, Joann Fedor, as high on meth. The sheriff then inspected the exterior and interior of the mobile home, finding nothing.

The disappearance of Louise remained unsolved for three years until Sheryl Baker had a crisis of conscience. She confessed to the crime, telling the authorities of what happened the day Louise was killed. In return for her confession, the authorities allowed her to plead to second-degree murder.

One of Louise's cousins stated on-line that the prosecuting attorney told her that one of trio involved admitted that they dismembered the body of Louise. They then spread the body parts out across different locations on different Indian reservations.

"For meth heads," Smith said. "They certainly knew what they were doing when disposing of a body. They were all jobless junkies but when it came to murdering someone they were willing to work hard. Damn hard in order to avoid detection. They would have avoided detection but for Sheryl Baker finally coming forward."

Kerry's trial would begin on February 8th, 1995. The judge, Thomas J. Whelan stated that

"I think the record is clear that nobody has ever been found in this case. The record is equally clear that there is circumstantial evidence that there was a homicide. There's also conflicting circumstantial evidence that it may not be a homicide; in fact, she may still be alive ..."

"My reason for making these statements is to establish for the record that in my mind corpus is a legitimate issue in this case. It's not a ruse that - there is a legitimate issue before the jury as to whether or not there's - a corpus of a homicide has been established."

Kerry would never confess to the crime on record and would claim innocence.

"The thing that makes me the most mad is that he is lying, and he knows he's lying," Kerry said of the prosecuting attorney.

The jury foreman, John Castleman, would concede that they found her guilty on the basis of "the type of murder it was" despite a lack of physical evidence to prove that Louise was murdered.

Mark Thompkins would be convicted of first-degree murder.

Kerry Dalton would be sentenced to death on May 23rd, 1995.

"She is the epitome of evil," Smith said. "We can say the drugs did it but there was a lot of premeditation to what she did to poor Louise. If anyone deserves to be on death row and have her execution expedited, it is Kerry Dalton."

Victoria Forbes, however, continues to champion the innocence of her sister.

"She was convicted without a body," Forbes said. "Without a weapon, without any blood evidence, without any physical evidence, without a crime scene, without anyone being declared deceased nearly seven years later as she stood trial with no one declared deceased being charged with the death penalty."

There continued to be some on-line controversy regarding Kerry's guilt as her supporters point to the fact that Louise's husband claims to have had a call from Louise a week after she was murdered.

That "evidence", however, is all they have to go on.

Despite Dalton's persistence at an appeal, it was clear to law officials believe that Kerry Dalton was guilty of the murder of Irene Louise May. Neither Tompkins nor Baker had anything to go after coming forward after three years of silence. They finally sobered up and confessed their crime.

Kerry Dalton did not and is now on death row.

SHEILA LABARRE

LORRAIN MOUNT

PROLOGUE

The farmhouse and surrounding area looked like something from the set of "Little House on the Prairie."

The house on Harvey Farm stood nestled in between tall pine trees, peaceful streams, and wildlife.

A place where you don't expect to find scenes that would be given an "X" rating if it were a horror movie.

The police arrived at the home while conducting a search for a missing young man named Kenneth Countje. They did not have to search far to find evidence of criminal activity. In the front of the property, lay a mattress burning alongside a smoking garbage barrel.

Their first inclination was to believe that the resident was burning garbage. A citation was due, maybe, but they had more pressing matters to attend to.

But upon closer inspection of the barrel, the officers saw a bone sticking out of the garbage.

A femur?

A mass of fleshy goo remained at the knob of the bone and the smell of the charred remains made the policemen gag.

They both gave each other a look of horror. Here in a town where the most serious crime would be a speeding ticket or jaywalking, the police were about to enter a whole world of horror beyond their wildest imagination.

CHAPTER ONE

Epping, New Hampshire.

Population = less than six thousand.

Epping is a rainy, small town that has been sarcastically nicknamed "The Center of the Universe". That has not stopped the residents from hosting parades, canoe races and music festivals. But when Sheila LaBarre arrived, the tiny hamlet soon became known for murder.

"She was a smart woman," forensic psychologist Paula Orange said. "Not book smart but intuitive. She could read people."

Sheila was born Sheila Kaye Bailey in Fort Payne, Alabama in 1958.

She was the youngest of six children. Her first marriage with a man named Ronnie Jennings would last less than two months. Jennings would find out that Sheila had been locking his child from a previous marriage in a closet to punish her. Jennings would divorce Sheila but she would find herself a new man in short order, tying the knot with John Baxter and moving to Chattanooga, Tennessee. Even though married, she would secretly fantasize about being swept away by a rich man. Sheila's mental illness would come to bear in her second marriage and that would end in divorce as well. Despondent, Sheila tried to kill herself and was sent to a psychiatric facility. She would be raped by an orderly inside the hospital.

Now single in Tennessee, the cash-strapped Sheila was forced to live in a local YMCA. She attended a church service and had a private talk with one of the preachers as she wanted "spiritual guidance." She would later claim that the reverend asked if she wanted to "sit in his lap." She then went to a psychiatrist who asked her if she had anal sex with any of her former husbands. The doctor then called Sheila at home and asked if "what she was wearing" and if she "was touching herself."

"If what we are to believe all of Sheila's stories," Orange said. "Then literally all of her interactions with men have ended with them as the pervert and her as the victim. Her sister would later testify that Sheila was molested by her father when she was young. Then her abusive marriages, the rape at the psych facility segues into a spiritual search where she meets a preacher who shows her the tent in his pants. Crazy."

CHAPTER TWO

Sheila turned to personal ads after her failures in marriage. She didn't like the normal courtship process of going to bars and meeting men there. She used the personal ads to cherry pick the men she wanted, men she could dominate.

"Whether on-line or off-line, Sheila behaved like a woman who was in complete control," Orange said. "She would develop a strange kind of power over men. It was almost as if she knew which men would be vulnerable to her feminine wiles and which ones would fight back. But when it came to Dr. Bill LaBarre, it was more of a case of getting the money."

While in Tennessee, Dr. LaBarre decided to take out a personal ad. He would get a response from Sheila who immediately sought to separate herself from the other paramours of the rich doctor.

She sent the doctor nude Polaroids of herself.

The strategy worked.

"She showed no shame in flirting with the older man and soon had him in the palm of her hand," Orange said. "He'd buy her fancy clothes, necklaces, the whole nine yards."

Wilfred "Bill" LaBarre was a successful chiropractor but lonely. Overweight and bespectacled, he had little to offer aside from his wealth. He was in his sixties and recently widowed.

Dr. Labarre was considered a good man by all who knew him. He had been the "Chiropractor of the Year" in 1983 but that would be the same year his beloved Edwina would pass away from cancer. Eager to salve the loneliness, he married another woman named Leona but she abandoned the doctor after a few years. He had two children from his first marriage; Laura and Gregory.

Now alone and widowed, the doctor wanted to spend his golden years enjoying his wealth.

And a young woman.

He would look at the nude Polaroids of the curvaceous Southern Belle, becoming obsessed.

"Here was a lonely, older man who all of a sudden had a 27-year old woman sending him nude photos. He thought he hit the jackpot."

Dr. LaBarre soon invited Sheila to come live with him at his farm in Epping, New Hampshire. The farm was a spacious one, a 115-acre horse ranch that according to LaBarre, "needed a female hand."

Sheila would become enamored by life on the farm, at least at first. She "never heard a June bug before" and the isolated country home gave her a peace that she never experienced.

Neighbors were not shocked that Dr. LaBarre took in such a younger woman as his girlfriend. He reportedly had other girlfriends after his wife died. "Sheila ran all the other girls off," one neighbor said.

But Sheila would prove to be a high-maintenance girlfriend. She would drain Dr. LaBarre's finances, making him buy her gifts and prizes which included a brand-new Silver Mercedes.

She also began to interject herself into LaBarre's estate and business dealings.

The farm that LaBarre owned was called the Old Harvey Farm. It was named after the original owners of the property who still lived in the area. But Sheila forced the doctor to change the name, she wanted it called something that reflected her personality.

The Silver Leopard Farm.

Sheila then had a sign made up and had it placed at the entrance.

She was marking her territory.

CHAPTER THREE

Despite the constant gifts and financial prizes, Sylvia proved to be an ungrateful sugar baby. The relationship would turn tempestuous after a few months. Sheila would claim that Dr. LaBarre often referred to himself as an "old fart" and looked the other way when Sheila began to have different men over for sex.

"He just worried about me when I would date far from home. But he was getting old and his heart would stop beating sometimes."

But the couple fought and police were routinely called to the residence to mediate their domestic disputes.

"You would sometimes hear gunshots," Bruce Allen, a LaBarre neighbor said. "You would hear her screaming, 'I'm going to kill you, you mother fucker!'"

Sheila once pulled a gun on the doctor and forced him out of the home. The chiropractor hid behind a boulder as his girlfriend shot at him.

LaBarre's daughter also recalled that she heard Sheila screaming threats at her father. "I'm gonna kill the horses and I'm going to kill you too."

Laura would later remark at how much her father changed after Sheila came into his life. He went from a normal, well-liked member of the community to a meek, submissive man.

"Sheila was all about being an opportunist," Orange said. "She had the ability to read a man, analyzing his weaknesses, size him up and then push the buttons. With LaBarre, she had a lonely man in front of her. He would tolerate anything in order not to lose her at first and then he simply became fearful of his life. These men in this small New England town did not have the wherewithal to deal with a violent sociopath like Sheila."

Sheila didn't stop with the renaming of Old Harvey Home. She soon took over the accounting duties at LaBarre's chiropractic business. She began organizing the practice into a well-oiled machine. She would track down patients who owed the doctor money and file numerous small claims in the Hampton District Court.

Concerned friends would advise him to dump Sheila before it was too late but it became apparent that the doctor either didn't know how or was afraid to. Dr. LaBarre informed neighbor Bruce Allen that he "had to get rid of her" and that he wanted to "send her back to Alabama. Hopefully, she'll stay there."

Her power over Dr. LaBarre increased to the point where he had given her power of attorney. She began rewriting his will, becoming the executor of his estate. The will stated that he was leaving everything to "a very special lady known as Sheila Kaye Jennings LaBarre."

"The will was very carefully redacted from the original," Orange said. "She kept a lot of the parts of the original and used her own typewriter to amend the little detail of where all the assets will go to. She was very astute and covered her tracks very well for someone who was supposedly schizophrenic."

The two would live together (Sheila would move out briefly but claim to be his common-law wife) from 1987 until LaBarre's death in 2000 at the age of 74. The coroner logged his cause of death as heart disease. There were suspicions among those close to the doctor that believe Sheila poisoned him to hasten the process.

"He was pretty old," Orange said. "And according to the autopsy, the heart disease was significant. So Sheila didn't have anything to do with his death despite the suspicions. The killings would come later."

Sheila would inherit the farm, LaBarre's Chiropractor office, two apartments and a rental home.

This was all valued at over two million dollars in assets.

Strangely, Sheila would marry a Jamaican national named Wayne Ennis in August of 1995 while living with Dr. LaBarre. Ennis drove a tour bus around Jamaica and Sheila made sure that when she toured the islands with Dr. LaBarre that they would cross paths with her Jamaican lover. She arranged for Ennis to obtain a visa and took him back to the farm with her. She would later claim that she and the doctor had stopped having sex and that she "had needs" which apparently Ennis took care of. She would later concede to pleasing the doctor sexually, "I'd use my hand," she said afterward.

Ennis would live in the farmhouse for almost a year. He had his own numerous encounters with Sheila which were violent and bizarre. One night, she ordered him to get in the car. The two then drove around the quiet town, Sheila's voice taking on a conspiratorial tone.

"I wish one of those damn horses would just kick him (Dr. LaBarre) in the head," Sheila said. "Kick him in the head and kill his old ass. I've thought about strangling him myself. But now I have a better idea. I want you to kill him."

Ennis was too frightened to say no to Sheila. The two would eventually divorce and the court records reveal that Sheila took out a restraining order against him.

Ennis disputed the allegations and stated that Sheila was the abuser.

He would later recall being punched, pushed, and shot at by Sheila.

"She told me that she was going to send me back to Jamaica in a box," Ennis said.

Dr. LaBarre told Ennis that Sheila was crazy and believed that she would eventually kill him. He gave the Jamaican money and sent him to the bus station, requesting that he leave town for his own safety.

After the relationship with Ennis ended, Sheila began dating James Brackett.

She and James would remain together for six years despite the fact that Sheila would attack Brackett with a pair of scissors, a machete, and an ax. When all of that failed she tried to shoot him.

The two would break up after which Brackett would get himself a vanity license plate that read "I'm Alive."

Brackett recalled moments where Sheila would act sweet and nice only to go into a violent rage moments later. He said that the greatest example was a time when he was taking a long bath with Sheila only to have her get out of the tub and smash him in the face with a two-foot grill brush.

Two of his teeth would be knocked out from the impact.

Sheila would attack Brackett for a variety of transgressions that would not be guilty of. Hurting her rabbits, damaging her property or having affairs with other women.

Brackett finally had enough, escaping from the farm on one rainy night and hitchhiking back into town.

"I'm lucky to be alive," he would later state.

CHAPTER FOUR

Sheila inherited the farm after LaBarre's death. The doctor's children tried to contest the will but were told that the odds of winning the case were 50/50 at best. They would also have to front over $50,000 to pay for the court costs.

Sheila soon turned the farm into her own private fiefdom. She would hire young men to help her around the place then pay them with her sexual favors or sometimes just beat the shit out of them.

"There would neighbors that would claim to see young men leave her house," Orange said. "They would look beaten up; black eyes, bloody lips, facial contusions. God knows what else."

Her neighbors began to suspect something fishy was going on but had no real evidence to call the police with.

"The first time I met Sheila LaBarre was at the Harvey Farm Stand," said Bonnie Meroth, one of Sheila's neighbors. "It was during the summertime when the produce was ready. I had no basic interaction with her except that of someone standing next to another person as a consumer. And she suddenly turned around and said 'I'll kill you if you come down to my farm' or words to that effect."

Bonnie would later claim that Sheila would try to scare her while driving down the road, nearly running her over while she was on her morning walk.

When she wasn't intimidating neighbors and townsfolk, Sheila would use the farm as the playground for her own private fetishes.

She liked to control and bully men. Stroking one of her pet rabbits, she would punish and insult the men unlucky enough to work at her farm.

"Are you kidding me?" Sheila yelled at the young man who dropped the wheelbarrow. "This should have been done yesterday."

He was young and naive, needing money. If it meant taking lip from Sheila, so be it. He needed work and she seemed nice when she hired him.

"Hurry up!" Sheila said, kicking the man in his buttocks. "Move, move. Are you kidding me? I've never seen a lazier man in my life."

Fatigued after working sixteen hours for seven days straight, the young man keeled over in exhaustion, dropping the wheelbarrow.

"Bitch made, perverted ass pedophile!" Sheila said. "Is this what I am paying you for? I am paying you to work. Now get off your bitch ass. Now!"

It became apparent that Sheila had a gift. A gift of controlling a certain type of man. Verbally abusive and overbearing, she encountered very little resistance.

She kicked the young man again. "Your name is 'bitch', you hear me?"

His real name was Michael Deloge.

CHAPTER FIVE

Deloge had problems as a teen. He got caught up in drugs and found himself on the streets, living out of homeless shelters. In 2004, he would meet Sheila LaBarre.

Deloge became smitten with the woman whom he saw as the life of the party. She would drink beer and play country songs on a guitar. According to Deloge's stepfather, Gordon Boston, the duo would indulge in drugs and study "sadistic material".

Deloge would join Sheila at her farm and soon become her personal whipping boy. Sheila would slap him around like a rag doll. One of the fellow ranch hands, Philip Sullos, recalled witnessing Sheila beating on Deloge with a hardwood stick until he bled. Deloge cowered and took the beating. She would then throw Deloge into a windowless shack and slam the door shut.

Deloge would cower meekly in the corner until Sheila came and got him, making no attempt to escape.

He would be declared missing in 2004 and no one would ever see him again.

In February of 2006, Sheila began looking for a new farmhand. She had her own criteria. He had to be young but pliable to her controlling methods.

She would find the perfect foil in Kenny Countie.

"Kenny was a lovely boy," Carolynn Lodge, Kenny's mother said. "He couldn't do enough for you. Everyone was his friend. I was so proud of him. He never had a horrible word for anybody and that was the problem. He trusted everybody."

Kenny's trust would lead him into Sheila LaBarre's trap.

Kenny would answer one of Sheila's personal ads. The young man was still naive and according to some reports had a "low IQ". The two met through a telephone personal ad service with Sheila calling up the young man and charming him in a way that no woman ever did.

"He (Kenny) told my son Brian that he met a 47-year old woman in New Hampshire," Lodge said. "She owned a farm. She owned a beautiful car. And she was rich. And he was serious about her."

"Kenny fit Sheila's psychological criteria," Orange said. "She targeted men whom she could overpower not only physically but also mentally. She was older than Kenny and light years more cunning. She knows exactly what to say and do to push his buttons. She takes the lead, telling him that he is going to be 'in for the time of his life' and that she 'can't wait to see him.' To a young man with limited experience and intelligence like Kenny, this is music to his ears."

Sheila would arrive at Kenny's home in the silver Mercedes. The silver leopard, the cougar, picking up her prey and taking him back to her lair.

Kenny's family would never see him again.

Sheila would use the same methods on Kenny as she did on the men in the past. She seduced the young man first then isolated him in her farmhouse. Then she berated him verbally before beating the shit out of him with face slaps, punches, and a wooden stick.

The beatings would come to a head during a weekend in February of 2000. Sheila beat Kenny's face into a pulp, took the wooden cane to his legs and may have poisoned him.

Then she decided to take him shopping at Walmart.

Placing him in a wheelchair, she rolled him around the outlet as she stocked up on garden supplies. She dumped two containers of diesel fuel into the prone Kenny's lap.

Little did he know that she would later use the gas to incinerate his body.

Customers gawked at the odd couple, concerned about the contusions on Kenny's face.

"Fuck you looking at?" Sheila would scream as she sped down through the aisle.

Employees of the store soon became concerned, calling the police.

The cops would arrive, confronting the couple in the store. They inquired about Kenny's condition but he didn't respond. Instead, Sheila took the lead, telling Kenny that he "didn't have to talk to these assholes."

The police didn't follow through. Kenny remained silent as Sheila rolled him through the store and out the door. No crime had been witnessed and they let the couple go.

Kenny's mother would later sue the police for negligence but it was tossed out of court in 2010.

A few nights after the Walmart incident, Sheila would make a frantic phone call to the police.

"I got a pervert in my house!" she screamed into the phone. "He's a pedophile! A pedophile!"

In a bizarre sequence of events, Sheila began to play a recording for the detective on the other end. She had routinely audio recorded everything she did, trying to incriminate the young men she worked with into admitting they were pedophiles. On this occasion, she played back a recording of her and Kenny.

"On the tape was my son, vomiting," Lodge said. "He kept saying 'he's faking, he's faking.'"

Sheila would ask Kenny if he was a pedophile on the tape. Kenny would answer 'yes'.

"Now he's a pedophile," Kenny's mother said. "Now he's raping children. Raping his brother. He's vomiting."

The police would write off the call as the rantings of a schizophrenic. They did not immediately respond to the residence.

Sheila would then kill Kenny Countie.

"She had to justify the killing of the young men in her own mind," Orange said. "For some bizarre reason, she would brainwash herself into thinking that her victims were pedophiles. She would repeat the question like a mantra, 'Are you a pedophile? Are you a pedophile?' Working herself up into an angry and violent state of mind before she killed the man."

Sheila's sister, Lynn Noojin, believed that Sheila was sexually abused by her father. Because of this, she became obsessed with child molestation. She would accuse the young men that worked for her of various sexual deviations, including pedophilia, incest, and bestiality.

CHAPTER SIX

After the bizarre call to police, authorities would not arrive at the farmhouse until the next morning. The police would enter the grounds, seeing both the burning mattress and barrel with Kenny's remains. They would not identify the burning bones as belonging to Kenny until much later.

Sheila had murdered Kenny the night before. She attacked Kenny ferociously with a kitchen knife, pushing the already weakened young man to the floor and stabbing away.

Blood sprayed and splattered everywhere.

Sheila then dragged Kenny's body out to her yard where she doused his body with the diesel fuel they had purchased at Walmart.

Lighting a match, she set the dead man on fire. She then took her pet rabbit in her lap, pulled up a chair and watched Kenny Countie burn.

"He was dismembered," Kenny's mother said, fighting tears. "And he was put in a pit and burned. But my son, he just wanted to be loved. I can't imagine what he must have been thinking. Because he was all alone."

Police would look throughout the house and find blood splatter on the walls and floor. A forensic team arrived and matched the blood with Kenny's DNA sample from his Army days. They would find the wallet of Michael Deloge but not his body.

Hundreds of police would spend seventeen days searching the 115-acre property. They found numerous burn pits and blood remains that were so old they had layers of dust on them. They would find clothing that belonged to Deloge and some toes that remain unidentified (it is rumored that the toes may belong to a mysterious Irish man who Sheila claims was stalking her.)

Going on the run from the cops, Sheila hitchhiked along Interstate 293. She was then picked up by Stephen Martello.

"Thanks so much for stopping," Sheila said.

"No problem," Martello said, looking the buxom Southern Belle up and down. His heart began to race.

Will he get lucky?

"My car broke down about two miles back. I got into a fight with my boyfriend and I'm trying to get to Dorchester."

"I'm headed that way," Martello said.

Sheila clutched her purse as if it were a security blanket and she kept looking back at the rear window.

"You all right?" he asked.

"Yeah," Sheila said "Just a little rattled. You know, it has been a tough day."

Martello took Sheila to the drug store when she said she needed to stop off and "buy some things". He tailed Sheila around the store until she bought a douche. Noting her erratic behavior, Martello disappeared out of Sheila's earshot to call the police on his cell phone.

"Hi," Martello said. "Just curious if you folks are looking for someone who just robbed a bank or an escaped mental patient. I just met a woman who is acting kind of strange."

When the authorities informed him that they were not actively investigating someone with that kind of background, Martello took Sheila to a hotel room.

The two would engage in wild and loud sex.

"You just had sex with an angel," Sheila proclaimed after they were done.

"Is that right?"

"You're not like the other men," Sheila said. "My boyfriend, Jesus, I just caught him with a huge stack of child porn. He is a pedophile. So are all those damn cops. Pedophiles, all of them. I think all sex offenders must die."

Martello said nothing. Instead, he put his pants and shoes on as fast as he could as Sheila continued to go on another bizarre rant.

"Vengeance is mine saith the Lord," Sheila said, laying on the bed in post-coital repose. "I was sent back to earth as an angel. I know how to speak to God in Hebrew. Do it every night."

Martello excused himself and high-tailed it out of the hotel room. He arrived home and saw the television broadcast about Sheila. He didn't call the police, worried that he would be an accessory to her crimes. Instead, Martello drove to the station and practically sprinted to the front desk.

"I think I just met Sheila LaBarre."

"To the end, Sheila had control over just about every man put in front of her," Orange said. "Here was a guy who picks her up at the side of the road. He thinks she is crazy enough to where he calls the cops to find out if there are any missing mental patients. He knows that she has a screw loose but he has sex with her anyway. It may be a poor reflection on men for sure but his response is typical. The men that Sheila encountered, from Dr. LaBarre all the way to Stephen Martello, all had the same false narratives going on in their head. They did not see a beautiful woman as something evil. It just didn't fit their narrative. So when Sheila begins her abuse, they just can't believe it. They refuse to hit a 'woman' back. She gets them 'pussy whipped' then beats the shit out of them. Rinse and repeat."

Sheila LaBarre would later be arrested for the murders of Michael Deloge and Kenneth Countje. She would plead no guilty on the grounds of insanity.

"This is a sick, sick woman," her attorney would argue. "Deeply disturbed."

Court-appointed psychiatrists would agree, testifying that Sheila was delusional as well as schizophrenic.

The jury would visit both LaBarre's farm and the Walmart where she frequented first hand. Sheila would join them as well although she was forced to wear a stun belt.

The jury did not buy her insanity defense and found her guilty.

"The fact that she has to remain for the rest of her life behind bars," Kenny's mother said. "She got what she asked for. She'll never see the light of day. Horrible thing is that my son, he's not here with me. He was only twenty-four."

Sheila LaBarre is now serving life in without possibility of parole.

BETTY LOU WILL KILL YOU

ALICE WILSON

Betty Lou Beets is a perfect historical example of how multifaceted crime can be, how a victim could become an aggressor, or an aggressor may adopt the mask of victimhood, and how all is not necessarily as it seems. Convicted for murdering two men and assaulting or attempting to kill four, Betty Lou's story is one that would send chills down the spine of any man from any era. Only the fourth woman to be executed for murder, despite the overall statistics hovering around forty to fifty cases of capital punishment per year, her crimes were too gruesome and cold for the court to offer her a lesser sentence... or were they? As we shall see when we delve into her history, despite Betty Lou's extensive criminal record and constant charges against her from ex husbands and her own children, the justice system was eager to give her a way out of the death sentence and allow her to live her natural life out in prison. And although there were some mitigating circumstances, it is telling that Betty Lou Beets almost got away with a life sentence in a situation where many others would have been executed without remorse.

Betty Lou Beets was born Betty Lou Dunevant on the 12th of March 1937, in Roxboro, North Carolina, USA. Her parents were initially tobacco farmers, whose main pleasure in life was alcohol, resulting in rampant alcoholism and a violent family life not atypical of the rural poor of the Great Depression. They lived on a diet of salt pork and various flours, barely touching vegetables or fruit, let alone eggs, fish, nuts or pulses, essential for developing a healthy brain and body. Furthermore, Betty Lou was disabled. She was not completely deaf, but hard of hearing due to having contracted the measles some time between the ages of three and six. Her fever was so severe and prolonged that she suffered damage to her brain and ears. As her hearing was affected at such a young age, she suffered an impairment to her speech similar to what many deaf or hard of hearing children suffer. At another time, or in another family, Betty Lou may have received treatment and hearing aids, but as a poor family in 1940, they could not afford to get her the treatment she would have needed to hear and speak normally. Her education was strongly impacted as she could not learn to read or study, resulting in borderline illiteracy and innumeracy and a frustrating life at home and away. Betty Lou also claimed she had been raped by her father in early childhood, as well as sexually abused by others. By the age of twelve her family life was falling apart. Her mother had been institutionalized due to breakdowns caused by alcoholism and Betty Lou had to drop out of school so she could care for her younger brother and sister. Her father, who seemed to see her as a surrogate mother for her siblings, became guarded against any sign of Betty Lou escaping and would beat her for not taking full responsibility for her siblings. She was often at the doctor's office or in hospital for the injuries he inflicted on her. She finally left school completely. The family moved to Hampton, Virginia, while Betty Lou was still a young girl, so that her father could work as a machinist. They were poor, she was young and disabled and she was a victim at the hands of the very people who were supposed to care for her. These circumstances were hardly the healthiest for the young girl to grow up in, and it is not shocking that Betty Lou became increasingly unstable and inclined to criminality in such an environment during such a time of deprivation. However it is also noteworthy that many more people suffered equal or worse hardship, yet did not turn to criminal activity. Perhaps it was the combination of everything, all together at once, but as she grew up something was going very, very wrong inside Betty Lou.

At the age of fifteen she married her first husband, Robert Franklin Branson. Far from an age where anyone feels quite ready to move into adulthood, Betty Lou was married for the first time. She would remain with him for seventeen years before finally divorcing. Although she levied accusations of violence against all her husbands, Robert Franklin Branson was the only one whose life she did not threaten directly herself. It appears he picked up where her father left off. If she was ever a unilateral victim, this may have been the one time. Within the first year she attempted suicide and became pregnant. They had a daughter together. She also later had a son with Robert Branson, who was also named Robert after his father. They went onto have four more children. Their children may have been a factor in reducing the marital violence, extending the duration of the relationship and, ultimately, saving Robert Branson Senior's life. In 1958 he evicted her from their home and put her on a bus to Virginia while he kept her children, at which point Betty again attempted suicide via an overdose of sleeping pills. They divorced in 1969, which left Betty Lou a financial and emotional wreck.

Being single took its toll on Betty Lou. She attached her self-worth to her ability to stay married. She began drinking to fight her feelings of loneliness. Between her own insecurities and the hard time she had getting money from either Robert Branson or the Welfare service to support her, Betty Lou soon felt she needed to remarry. She married Billy York Lane at the age of thirty two. Their marriage was a tumultuous one, and very short. There was evidence of mutual violence and disregard for each other's wellbeing. Lane had been abusive towards a previous partner and Betty Lou responded to his violence in turn. Her daughters recall how he used to beat her senseless and how she used to attack him. He initially wanted to charge her for attempted murder, but swiftly dropped the charges after he was forced to admit he had attacked her, broken her nose and threatened her life. They divorced the same year and remarried again shortly after the trial. After Betty Lou shot at him, Billy York Lane divorced her again, only a month after their remarriage, this time for good. It would prove the wisest decision of his life, as her subsequent husbands found out.

Betty Lou remained single for a year and unmarried for eight more years. During the interim Betty Lou worked in a warehouse, then took up work at a topless bar to cover the bills. She sent two of their children back home to Branson, as she could not afford to care for them. She went on to marry Ronnie C. Threlkold, her boyfriend of seven years, at the age of forty. However this relationship would be as unpredictable, violent and dangerous for Ronnie as it was for Billy. In this case there was little evidence Ronnie had been violent towards Betty Lou, although she accused him of violence at later dates, but her habits had been firmly cemented and she continued to display abusive behaviour towards him. She also continued to work at the topless bar, resulting in arrests and thirty days in country jail under the charge of public lewdness. Despite their seven year courtship, the marriage lasted just a year, culminating in Betty Lou Beets's attempted homicide of Ronnie in 1978, where she shot him in the stomach, wounding him, and their divorce in 1979.

She married Doyle Wayne Barker at the age of forty one, closely after her divorce from Threlkold. Their marriage lasted a mere seven weeks before her violent behaviour drove Doyle away from her. However his own violence was undeniable. He had stalked her, assaulted her and raped her during their short relationship. The day he left Betty Lou had bruises all over her face, neck, arms and chest. There is no available record of the divorce, however all living parties assumed it had taken place. However Doyle Wayne did not get out of their marriage unscathed. He disappeared after their divorce and his body was found years later, buried under a garage, killed by three gunshots.

But this grisly deed was not uncovered for many more years to come. Rather, Betty Lou went on to marry a firefighter named Jimmy Don Beets, her final husband, at the age of forty four.

"Jimmy Don Beets was a wonderful man," said a family friend. "He was loved by so many people. An old country boy that a lot people had respect for."

Their courtship would last a mere six months. Betty Lou would meet Jimmy while she worked as a waitress and the seduction began. Her two sons moved in with them. This would be her final marriage, and her actions within it would be her undoing. Although their courtship had been pleasant, they both suffered from alcoholism, which slowly drove their marriage to the same violence she had experienced previously. Less than a year later she murdered him by gunshot, and this time she was caught. Robert Branson, her son from her first marriage, had been informed that she intended to kill her last husband, telling him to steer clear of the residence as the murder took place. On the 6th of August 1983, Robert Branson Junior left their home and Betty Lou Beets committed the gruesome act. Not only did Robert provide evidence that the act was premeditated, but he also was expected to participate. Two hours after leaving the house, Robert Branson Junior returned, finding his step father dead with two gunshot wounds in his body. Rather than seek assistance, Robert Branson Junior, either tainted by a lifetime with a mother who viewed abuse and murder as daily events or himself an individual with low empathy, helped his mother to dispose of the body. Betty Lou Beets and Robert Branson Junior carted Jimmy Don Beets' body outside to an ornamental wishing well that stood in the front yard of their house. Undetected, they cast the body inside.

Then, Betty Lou returned to the house to cover up her acts. She called the police to report her husband missing from their Cedar Creek Lake home. The next day, Betty Lou became more devious. Perhaps inspired, perhaps unnerved by her success killing Doyle Wayne Barker, she realized she needed to create a story with which to divert the police from her trail. Robert Branson Junior recalled to the press how she had taken some of Jimmy Don Beets's heart medication down to his boat at the lake. Then she had removed the propeller, placed the medication in the boat and abandoned it, floating loosely in the water. Later that day, as the twenty four hours since Jimmy Don Beets's initial disappearance drew to a close, various officials began the search for the presumably missing man. Officers from the Henderson County Sheriff's department, various members of the fire department, as well as agents from the Texas Parks and Wildlife department searched for three weeks. They naturally found no body. However they did find Jimmy Don Beets's boat drifting in the lake, near to the Redwood

Beach Marina. There they found his fishing license, an unused life jacket and the heart medication which Betty Lou Beets had placed there. Not knowing anything about the murder or the forged evidence, they brought Betty Lou Beets to the Marina as the sole witness, where she identified the boat and its contents as those of her husband. Although no body had been recovered, it was considered case closed.

Betty Lou Beets would have likely got away with both murders, were it not for confidential information given to the Henderson County Sheriff's Department two years later. The information suggested that Jimmy Don Beets had not disappeared innocently, and that his assumed death, with no body that had been found, may be the result of foul play. The evidence was enough that the cold case was reopened in Spring 1985. As their suspicions became stronger, the investigators were drawn to Betty Lou Beets, who was arrested on the 8th of June of 1985 and then booked into the Henderson County Jail. An officer on the case, Rick Rose, who had been in charge of her arrest warrant, secured a further warrant to search the Beets's home and lands, including the yard. Ultimately, they discovered Jimmy Don Beets's remains buried under the wishing well where he had been left two years prior. But another discovery would surface that would further disturb the case. Also in the back yard was a storage shed which could be moved. When the officers moved it, something compelled them to disturb the soil that had lain there several years. Perhaps it was some confidential evidence or perhaps it was just intuition, but it paid off when they discovered a second body. Doyle Wayne Barker, still missing, was buried there, with three bullets in his body. All five bullets matched the .38 caliber pistol which had been seized from their home after another incident of Betty Lou's violent outbursts. Thanks to the calls she had made the very day of his disappearance there was no room to argue that she had been abusing drugs or alcohol at the time, but there had been no physical evidence that suggested to detectives at the time that Jimmy Don had been abusing her when the incident took place. Her position was weak.

Faced with the evidence, Robert Branson Junior and his sister Shirley finally confessed to their awareness of the killings, as well as their hand in the crimes that had taken place. Not only had Betty Lou told her son about the murder, but she had also informed her daughter, by the Shirley Stegner and not living at the family home, that she planned on killing her husband. Shirley was motivated by her confession to also confess to her involvement in another crime. She told the detectives that she had been involved in the burial of Doyle Wayne Barker's body in October of 1981 after Betty Lou had shot him to death.

In an effort to make herself more likeable to the jury, Betty Lou Beets raised her history of domestic violence as an excuse for her violent behaviour, levying charges against all her prior husbands, as well as her father. However, this would be the first that anyone had heard of most of these charges. This may have been due to attitudes of the times, a desire to protect her children, or the apparently two-sided nature of most of these incidents, however the jury would not believe her claims. They were just too convenient. Instead, it was clear to them that Betty Lou Beets was an unstable and dangerous woman and the only connection between the five men she married and their violence. Whatever the situation was, her psychological well being was never considered during the trial. Despite the obvious impact her upbringing and life would have on her mental state and the fact that her actions up until that point were indicative of definite mental illness, the trial system of the time did not account for that.

Furthermore, the premeditated nature of her actions was evident through her children's abundant testimonials, where they confessed she had shared her intent to kill not only the husbands she managed to murder, but that she had expressed a desire to kill all the men she had been married to. Not only that, but her success concealing the bodies, under the wishing well and under the garden shed, showed a lack of remorse and serious consideration of her crimes. However it seems Betty Lou had not been as careful as she thought. As soon as the trial began, various other witnesses emerged to testify against her. Various people recalled her attempting to collect life insurance of over a hundred thousand dollars as well as a pension of over a thousand dollars a month after Jimmy Don's declared death. A year after the official death of Jimmy Don Beets, she successfully sold his boat, the primary evidence that he had disappeared. She claimed she did not know about his pension or insurance, however seeing as Jimmy Don Beets was already retired and claiming his pension, this claim fell short. Furthermore, had she no awareness of them she would not have pursued either so actively. She claimed she had been told about them when she visited an attorney by the name or E. Ray Andrews about a fire insurance claim she needed to make, at which point he discovered she could claim his insurance and pension. However her own filing for these benefits did not align with the supposed visit, and the only person who could say for sure that she had not known about her deceased husband's finances was E. Ray Andrews himself, who agreed to represent her in exchange for the rights to book and movie deals concerning her life and case.

Betty Lou Beets was indicted for murder for remuneration or the promise of remuneration, with her recovery of his life insurance and pension as evidence. She plead not guilty and was taken to trial, where she was found guilty of the capital offence of first degree murder on the 11th of October of 1985. She was found again guilty during a hearing on the 14th of October 1985 and was sentenced to death by the trial court. This was due to her prior history of violence and attempted murders, which suggested that she would present a threat to others in the future, specifically to any man who entered a relationship with her again. Yet her conviction and sentence were quickly and successfully appealed to the Texas Court of Criminal Appeals. Such was the situation that, under Texas law, crime for the sake of insurance and pension claims was not covered by the definition of "murder for remuneration", instead falling into two separate categories of first degree murder and insurance fraud, or crime with intent to commit insurance fraud. The Texas Court of Criminal Appeals reversed her conviction for capital murder, citing the Texas Penal Code as evidence that her particular case could not be filed as "murder for remuneration". The State then requested a rehearing of the cause. Although her original conviction had been overturned, the fact remained that Betty Lou Beets was guilty of homicide under some circumstance or another.

On the 21st of September of 1988, the Court of Criminal Appeals reinstated her conviction and sentence based on the evidence received. Betty Lou Beets was on death row. Her execution was scheduled for the 8th of November 1989.

However her court case did not go as it should have in the first place. Attorney E. Ray Andrews was heavily invested in sensationalizing her case as much as he could, seeing as he would profit enormously from the case blowing up into a media phenomenon. So although she claimed and he later agreed that she had known nothing of her husband's finances, the trial was conducted under the assumption that she was fully aware of the money she would receive. Not only that, but E. Ray Andrews did everything in his power to create a more dramatic case on both sides, which ultimately meant excluding Betty Lou from much of the information about her own trial. Betty Lou was becoming desperate at this point. Although she had a long history of domestic violence, attempted murder and two bodies in her garden, she decided to attempt to blame the murder of Jimmy Don Beets on Robert Branson Junior, her own son. She did not seem to have made the statement in sound mind, but E. Ray Andrews allowed her to speak on her own behalf and did not retract it, as it added dramatic quality to the event. He tried to cover up later, saying that Betty Lou had possibly been taking the blame for her son, however he had no proof other than that Robert Branson Junior was male and from a rough background. This statement and its acceptance horrified the court, as it was alarming to them to see a mother who, rather than protect her children, was willing to throw them under the bus by falsely accusing them of a crime she had more than evidently committed. Furthermore, by admitting and adhering to the story that Robert Branson Junior was in fact the actual killer, Betty Lou lost all chances of arguing that she acted in self-defence and made her own accusations of domestic violence against Jimmy Don and her prior husbands completely irrelevant. This is despite the fact that a leading domestic violence specialist of the time believed Betty Lou Beets had been significantly mentally impacted by her experiences, and that she suffered "the emotional, cognitive, and behavioural components of battered woman syndrome, rape trauma syndrome, and PTSD" which he added must have interacted with her pre-existing organic brain damage from her childhood illness, history of battering and substance abuse. All together, this would have presented a robust case for her mental illness and need for treatment rather than punishment. However E. Ray Andrews discarded this option in favour of the more dramatic choice of supporting Betty Lou's accusation against her son. They became stuck in the position of having to argue she did not kill her husband at all. This context may have reduced her sentence, or made her eligible to claim insanity. However neither of these options were available.

Throughout the entire case, E. Ray Andrews failed to represent her seriously and did nothing to prevent her from shooting herself in the foot repeatedly. In fact, seeing the case was a lost cause and that he stood to gain more from her sentence than her freedom, Andrews began drinking heavily for the duration of the trial. He chose not to bear witness to her claims that she did not know about Jimmy Don Beets's pension or insurance, which would have transformed the case to one of murder in the context of domestic violence, rather than murder for remuneration. He managed to offer the jury no reasons to consider that Betty Lou was not a serious threat to those around her, eventually sealing her fate. Yet he remained her attorney for the duration of her appeal as well. It was he who raised the point that her financial gain was not necessarily the motivator for murder, but a by product. He also finally raised that she was not aware of the insurance or pension until she spoke to him, however this was met with scepticism due to his negligence to mention it any sooner, and was perceived as a lie in effort to overturn Betty Lou's criminal charges after his initial failure to protect her.

On the 16th of October 1989, Betty Lou filed a motion called a stay of execution which would delay her execution to give her time to prepare and file a habeas corpus application with the state. On the 1st of November she filed the application and the trial court delayed her execution so that the claims she was raising, such as consideration towards her mental state and marital conditions, could be properly addressed. During this time Betty Lou wrote several letters from prison in which she attempted to defend her good name and that of her last husband. She attempted to balance the accusations that she was a black widow by reminding the court that she was Jimmy Don's fourth wife as well. However his previous wives did not come forward to support her. She also defended her own identity, denying that she ever worked as a barmaid, regardless of her own charges for lewd behaviour, and that she was never on welfare, despite her claims after her first divorce. She also said that the Fire Department Chaplain, who stated he had informed her about Beets's insurance and pension, had spoken to her sister in law, Betty Beets, instead. She even quibbled over the descriptions of her garden, insisting the well was a planter in the shape of a well and not an actual well. It was clear that Betty Lou Beets was desperate to save face and project a more pleasant, more ordinary identity than the one which E. Ray Andrews had created for her in the courtroom. It was also clear that her mental health was degrading as she endured life in prison and submitted her habeas corpus petition. In her petition she argued against her sentence of the death penalty, raising issues such as the alleged value Jimmy Don Beets apparently added the community, the testimonials of victims and sufferers whose statements were unconstitutional under the Victim Impact Statements act of 1987, and the poor assistance which E. Ray Andrews provided, especially regarding her history of domestic abuse. Yet without his help in writing and presenting the letter, her claims were weak and not fully backed by legal evidence. Andrews did not visit her from the point of her sentencing and prepared for her trials without ever speaking to her. Furthermore, she could have claimed that his services were provided against American Bar Association rules, which prohibit the trade of legal services for copyright issues, such as the rights to her case. None of this was raised by her against him, and as such it was not considered during her habeas corpus appeal.

However on the 27th of June her appeal for state habeas corpus was turned away. She was placed in the position of proving that, had E. Ray Andrews presented a testimony about her lack of awareness of the insurance and her history of domestic violence, the jury would have judged her not guilty of a capital crime. Without a proper attorney to defend her, it would be impossible for Betty Lou to prove this was the case, and the court deemed Andrews's mistakes to have been harmless to her trial. The Fifth Circuit Court of Appeals went on to turn down her final appeals. The judges remained convinced that, regardless of any remaining evidence, Betty Lou Beets's history of violence and attempted murder, along with the two concealed bodies in her garden, were evidence enough that a death sentence was a fair response to the crime that had taken place. She had displayed violence her whole life, even towards men who had not presented a threat to her, and had attempted to kill all but one of her husbands. She had concealed her murders carefully and for many years and was willing to place the blame on her own adult son. In other words, regardless of her own situation, her criminal intent was viewed as evident and incorrigible, and her death sentence was the only fitting end to her crime spree.

On death row, Betty Lou Beets retained some supporters, mostly her own children. Some of Betty Lou's daughters went to E. Ray Andrews with photographic evidence of the domestic abuse she had suffered in order to request a parole review, but were declined. They insisted on presenting the evidence that she had suffered and that her acts of violence were a result of brain damage and abuse, not of malicious intent. Faye Lane, one of her daughters, insisted that her mother would only have done anything so horrific if she believed she was abused. Domestic violence awareness groups and charities acting against the death sentence appealed to have her sentence changed to a life sentence in prison, based not only on her own suffering, but on their universal stance against the irreversible process of the death penalty. Yet even those defending her maintained that she was a violent, unpredictable woman and not safe to exit into the general public.

And not all her children were so kind. Shirley told the press that Doyle Wayne Barker was killed because he owned the trailer where they lived, and that after the divorce which Barker had initiated, Betty Lou and her children would be evicted from the trailer and left homeless. This set a precedent where even her own daughter could not believe that Betty Lou was completely unaware of the financial benefits of murdering Jimmy Don Beets, especially not after she had successfully killed Barker. Knowing that she was still doubted and seeing hope as ever distant, Betty Lou composed her memoirs from death row, presenting her case.

Beets turned to her last resort which was to appeal to then-governor George W. Bush to spare her life. After a media incident where he jokingly insulted the last woman to be executed in Texas in an insensitive manner, George W. Bush seemed keen to prove he had no bias against women, even in the prison system, and agreed to review her case. This would have meant hearing the witnesses which had not been heard by the trial lawyer and present a case against her execution based on the circumstances of her life, including medical and psychiatric evidence. He could have granted her a thirty day reprieve in which he made his decision, however this never materialized. His number was made available and he received thousands of calls and letters from people urging him to spare her, with only fifty seven endorsing her sentence. Yet he did not grant the reprieve or halt the execution.

Betty Lou Beets was finally executed on the 24th of February of 2000, via lethal injection. Protestors from various organisations gathered outside as her sentence awaited. She declined both her last meal and her final statement, having been given by then enough time to make sense of what was happening and to say everything which needed to be said. Strapped to the death chamber gurney, she received her injection at six pm and died within eighteen minutes. She was sixty two years old. She left behind five adult children, nine grandchildren and six great-grandchildren, as well as her memoirs. Her story may be shocking, and it may be hard to pick sides at times, but that is exactly why her trial presents a solid case against the black and white ideals the court system held regarding crime and punishment, perpetrator and victim, defence and offence. Someone can at once be a victim of horrific crimes and a perpetrator of them, at once be a defendant and raise accusations, at once deserve punishment yet suffer a crime gone unpunished. There is no doubt that Betty Lou Beets was a violent woman who invited violence into her own life, an alcoholic and a murderer. However there is no doubt either that she was a good mother within her capacity, a victim of a series of horrific crimes, a disabled person with a background she could not escape and a desperate woman who saw no way out of her situation. Neither black nor white, good not bad, Betty Lou Beets sits in the grey areas of the law.

THE REAL GONE GIRL : THE TRUE STORY OF MICHELLE THEER

71

DARLA PUGH

At first glance, Michelle Theer looked like the stereotypical bored housewife. She married an Air Force captain who was deployed on assignment for long periods of time. Her days were spent alone and idle.

And you know what they say about idle hands.

Michelle felt unfulfilled in her marriage and didn't so much want out, she wanted something more. Attractive with long brown hair and arched eyebrows, Michelle did not have any problems attracting members of the opposite sex. She needed something discreet, however, something that would simply titillate her fantasies and relief the boredom that she would suffer during the long absences of her husband.

So she turned to the Internet.

It started innocently at first. A few keystrokes of flirtatious messages. Some a bit racier than others, but where was the harm? She was hiding behind a computer monitor. It isn't cheating if there is no face to face, Michelle thought.

Then she came across the profile of John Diamond. His pictures showed him to be a tall and muscular man, a special forces soldier that made Michelle's heart skip a beat.

Or maybe she saw him as the perfect foil. The perfect fall guy to get rid of her husband.

Their flirtations started innocently enough. Then the messages got racier and racier until they both felt the need to satiate their fantasies for one another.

Those fantasies led to sex.

Then murder.

Frank Theer, better known as "Marty", was a quiet and reserved young man. In high school, his friends introduced him to what they believed what be his perfect match.

Michelle Forcier.

Michelle was outgoing, bubbly and only sixteen when she met Marty who was a year older. Her friends believed that Michelle's extroverted personality could be a counterweight to Marty's introverted nature. Marty had originally intended to become an astronaut, his ambition and intelligence made him an attractive catch to Michelle. They were both the product of military families, both moving a lot as children so they had a kinship there. Both were ambitious and had concrete plans for the future. Marty would join the Air Force. Michelle would join the reserves and serve in the Gulf War.

"Michelle had ambition," forensic psychologist Paula Orange said. "She wanted status and respect. But she grew up in a military family and succumbed to the tribalism and social pressures that existed in that kind of environment. You grow up, get married and have kids. Michelle probably had mixed feelings about that. She wanted to do her own thing. So, in essence, she was living a double life from the get-go. She was doing the expected thing of getting married but on the side she was the libertine, drinking heavily and having extra-marital affairs."

The couple would maintain their long-distance relationship for four years until Michelle was assigned to the

Persian Gulf War in 1991. Thinking that their courtship had lasted long enough, Marty asked Michelle to marry him.

Michelle, at twenty years old, said yes to the other man she had known up until that point.

Their wedding video would show the couple to be a happy one. They kissed for the cameras and fed each other wedding cake.

"We did everything together," Michelle said. "He treated me really well. I just thought we had the perfect relationship. We were best friends."

The couple would remain married for six years as Marty's Air Force assignments forced them to move from base to base. Michelle had fantasized about going to exotic locations overseas. Instead, Marty's tenure was limited to uninspiring outposts in Oklahoma, Alabama and Florida.

Places that would bore Michelle to tears.

"Michelle was getting lonely," Orange said. "Like so many military families, these things take shape early on. Marty would be gone months at a time and of course telephone and e-mail exchanges are not the same as a face to face. Michelle felt entitled to more from life then what she was getting. This isn't uncommon obviously but Michelle took things one step further eventually."

During the occasions when Marty was on leave, he and Michelle would often end up fighting.

"I want children," Marty said.

"No way," Michelle would shake her head, stifling a laugh.

"Then what's the point? What's the point of being married if we are not going to start a family?"

"Raise children in this shithole? You've got to be kidding."

The arguments would escalate. Michelle was a slob, refusing to clean up around the house. Marty would complain but Michelle would deflect and criticize him for his poor career choice.

"You're never home," Michelle hissed. "And you want a family?"

After nine years of marriage, Marty was sent to the Pope Air Force Base near Fayetteville, North Carolina. Fayetteville was considered to be the equivalent of Siberia when it came to transfers. Military members gave the town nicknames like FayetteNam, Fatalville, and FayetteHell. Michelle found the town to be even worse than its reputation when it came to providing excitement.

"Here I was in Fayetteville," Michelle said. "'Loserville'. And I had nobody I could hang out with. Nobody I could pick up a phone and call."

Marty saw things differently, writing on a Christmas card in 2000, "Pope has provided a great change of pace for me and Michelle is happy with her new job. So, 2000 is looking good for both of us."

Michelle would suffer from depression and loneliness after the six years of marriage. Marty tried hard to appease his high-maintenance wife. He took her scuba diving in the

Caribbean, skiing in the Rockies, parachuting in Georgia and then a summer marathon run in Alaska.

Despite all of the adventures, Michelle was dissatisfied. She wanted something more out of life, more excitement. She decided to go back to school and earn a degree in psychology. She felt desperately alone, however, as Marty would once again be deployed overseas. Michelle would find work with a psychologist named Dr. Thomas Harbin's and work to obtain her license in psychology.

Still, it wasn't enough. She needed excitement.

More specifically, sexual excitement.

So she turned to the Internet.

Michelle began turning to dating sites. She noodled around with different memberships and it never became more than an idle pursuit to fill the hours of loneliness. Setting up her ad with the headline of "sexy brunette seeks rendezvous man", her inbox was immediately deluged with drooling suitors.

She entertained a number of different men, sending and receiving flirty messages. Michelle had become interested in the local "swinger" and sex club scene, advertising for a man who would be her escort to a club called "Carolina Friends."

One man got her attention more than the others.

JOHN DIAMOND

John was four years younger than Michelle, entering the United States Army during the year in which the couple got married. He had a wandering eye, currently married to his second wife knew of his lothario ways. She was a Panamanian woman who was a few years older than John. He didn't hide his infidelities and on one occasion had one of his girlfriends call the house to ask his wife if John was still meeting her at the beach.

"John loved women," Debbie Dvorak, John's younger sister said. "He loved women, he always had a girlfriend and was a ladies man. My brother was an attractive guy. He had a great personality. His personality made him that much more attractive."

John's background was remarkably similar to Marty in that he was born into a military family. His father was a Vietnam veteran and his grandfather had been a POW during World War II. John himself became an Army ranger and was stationed nearby at Fort Bragg. He was trained as a sniper and highly decorated. Their military backgrounds were where their similarities ended, however. Marty was highly respected as a pilot and a family man. John was a good soldier but nowhere near the honorable family man Marty was.

"John was a highly regarded soldier," Orange said. "But he already had two families. He had a child with his first wife and they divorced. He remarried and had a son with the second wife. So his plate was already full by the time he met Michelle Theer."

John and Michelle both intuitively knew what the other wanted. They both needed the adrenaline, the excitement of forbidden sex to add spice to their humdrum lives. John and Michelle spent months sending each other flirtatious and juicy e-mails before realizing it was time to put fantasy aside and meet for real.

There was an immediate attraction as they met at a Fayetteville coffee shop.

"It was love at first sight," John said.

"I thought he was very, very charming," Michelle said. "He was funny. We talked about movies and music. Things that me and Marty didn't talk about."

They were both still married, however, and that added to the thrill.

LET THE SEDUCTION BEGIN

John and Michelle then began spending as much time with they could with one another. Their extra-marital affair could be done inside Michelle's own bedroom as Marty would be stationed overseas. Michelle grew addicted to the sex, the excitement and the adoration that John gave her.

"He was very attentive," Michelle said. "He was very affectionate. He was very adoring. Yeah, it felt great."

The sex grew addicting for both John and Michelle. Like drug addicts, they found escape through the pleasures of the flesh. E-mails and text messages between the two would reveal a controlling relationship that favored Michelle. He was at her beck and call, like a "puppy dog" said one investigator.

"I can't wait until you come back so we can take care of each other," John wrote in one message. "You know, sex, sex, sex and of course...more sex. I know that we are meant to be together and are kindred soul mates. I will always love you, no matter how you have hurt me."

"I think it was just the sex," Dvorak said when asked what John saw in the married Michelle. "He was obsessed. He was smitten with having sex with her."

Michelle would later reveal to her psychologist that she didn't think that the affair took away from her love for Marty.

"She said that Marty was the love of her life," Orange said. "With John, it was just lust. She never loved him the same way she loved Marty. At least that is how she differentiated and rationalized it in her mind."

Without fear of being caught, the two began going to dance clubs as well as "swinger parties" as a couple at Michelle's request.

"She would take him to these sex clubs," Dvorak said. "She would say 'If you want to go have sex with her, that's okay. That's fine. Go. I'm fine with it.' And he was just like 'Wow, okay.'"

Finding a partner in crime for her sex addiction, Michelle indulged whenever she could.

Then Marty returned home.

REPAIR JOB?

Marty had been undergoing flight maneuvers in Little Rock, Arkansas. When he returned home to Fayetteville, he came back knowing that his marriage was on the rocks. Michelle wanted to go to marriage counseling but Marty refused.

"He wouldn't agree to marriage counseling and I moved out," Michelle said. "He was shocked."

Michelle got her own place that summer. She would spend most of her days and nights in the arms of John Diamond. "He was so attentive," Michelle recalled. "He would rub my feet for five hours if I wanted him to."

John continued to fall deeper in love with Michelle. He thought that she was more intelligent than the women he had dated before, more of a challenge. Three months after living alone, however, Michelle changed her mind about John.

She went back to Marty.

Michelle thought she would give the marriage one more chance. Marty relented on going to counseling and the couple hashed things out with the therapist.

"I want Michelle to clean up around the house more," Marty said to the counselor. "I mean, I know that with women's lib and all that sounds very degrading. But I work my tail off. I'm away for months at a time and would at least like to come home to someplace clean. It shows respect. Coming home to a mess of a house shows a lot of disrespect."

"See what I mean?" Michelle said. "Talk about obsessive-compulsive. Where does a clean house fit in the grand scheme of things? I want to live life. Go out and have new experiences. But this guy? All he wants to do is stay home. Stay home in his clean house."

The counseling didn't work. In the summer of 2000, Michelle moved out of the family home. She and John found an off-base apartment and began living together. The cheating couple took a vacation to the Netherlands Antilles and fell in love with the place. Michelle enjoyed it so much that she applied to the Saba School of Medicine. She listed John as her next of kin, describing his relationship to her as "fiancee".

But later Michelle would tell her psychologist that her decision to go back with John was a "relapse."

"I knew that I loved Marty," Michelle said. "And I knew that I wanted to make it work. I knew it in my heart."

Then she went back to Marty again.

She continued to see John, however, but the relationship would be on and off. John would plead his case through e-mails, writing flowery messages about how much he loved Michelle.

"I love you so much," John wrote. "I know you feel the same. What I don't understand is how you could be with a man that you don't love anymore. You're unhappy with him. You're happy with me. This is all so confusing."

"He said specifically 'I'm going to kill myself,' Michelle said. "'I can't live without you. You can't do this to me. I'm gonna go drive my car off a bridge.'"

According to Michelle, John would not relent in his pursuit of her. He would show up at her office and make a scene, telling her that he would tell Marty about their affair.

Michelle relented to seeing John one last time, agreeing to meet with John at a local restaurant. According to her statements to her psychologist, she went there in the hopes of ending the affair for good.

"We had that whole talk," Michelle said. "You know, 'we can only be friends' and 'this can never happen again. Never, never, never.' He seemed very calm. Very rational. I told him, 'I don't want to leave my husband.' I never told him, 'I love you.' I never said 'I want to be with you.' I mean, I think I was pretty straight up."

Whether this conversation took place or not, it certainly landed on deaf ears to John. He continued to pursue Michelle and they continued to see one another.

"She probably led him on a roller coaster ride of emotions," military investigator Vincent Bustillo said. "Brought him to the peak, thinking everything was going to be good and they're going to leave this life together, off in some Caribbean island, and then back off and leave Diamond emotionally distraught to the point where that's what he wanted and nothing was going to get in his way."

The on-again, off-again relationship turned red hot by December 9th, 2000. Michelle told Marty that she would be attending a birthday party for a graduate school friend of hers. Thinking nothing of it, Marty simply nodded his head.

Michelle left the home and met John for a night of torrid sex.

"The manipulation began early on in the relationship," Orange said. "Michelle would pull John into her world with sex. Then she would push him away by going back to her husband. John was smitten with her and could not let go.

He would have done anything for her and Michelle knew it. An Army ranger willing to do anything for you is a powerful thing. It was like having her own personal soldier willing to kill. But who did she need getting rid of and why?"

Michelle knew that Marty had a half-million dollar insurance policy that he took out in 1999.

She was the sole beneficiary.

John's sister, however, remained adamant that Michelle had written those lovelorn letters to herself in order to put the trail on John Diamond.

"He never once expressed any feelings of love for her to me," Debbie Dvorak said. "Unless you come to me with a handwritten letter that he was obsessed with her, I'll never believe that. He told me he did not want to marry her. He did not want to spend the rest of his life with her. I think she was obsessed with him. Obsessed that she couldn't control him. That she couldn't control the situation."

Eight days later after her latest rendezvous, Michelle would attend a Christmas party given by her employer, Dr. Thomas Harbin. She brought along Marty who seemed to enjoy the company at the otherwise mellow party. About an hour into the get-together, Michelle excused herself to make a phone call.

A phone call to John Diamond.

A short while later, Marty and Michelle drove another couple home before heading to the local gas station.

"We ended up turning around and going back to the office," Michelle said. "To get some stuff that I needed so I could stay up and work that night."

Marty sat in their Ford Explorer and watched as Michelle walked up to the second story office. A few minutes passed and Marty got worried. He got out of the car and went upstairs to her office to make sure his wife was okay.

He reached the top of the stairs and then he was ambushed.

A gunman stepped out from the shadows and fired four times. Marty tumbled down the stairwell. When he reached the bottom, he was still alive.

The shadowy gunman stood above him and fired one more time, killing Marty.

Michelle would state to police that she discovered Marty's body and began screaming his name. She said that she thought he was still breathing but in the haste of living her office she locked her keys inside. Michelle said she ran two miles to a video store to call 911 despite the area having numerous homes and businesses nearby.

Police arrived on scene and found Michelle cradling Marty in her arms, her husband's blood pooling onto the concrete. Military police arrived shortly after the city authorities, getting the case after it was revealed that Marty was an Air Force Captain.

Both police agencies initially suspected that Marty was the victim of a random robbery. They searched the area and found no one despite the fact that Michelle stated that she has "seen someone in the bushes" when she discovered Marty's body.

FIGURING THINGS OUT

Investigators would discover bullet holes at the top of the stairwell as well as sequins from Marty's suit. They surmised that Marty was at the top of the stairwell when he was shot from someone coming from the bottom of the steps. He then fell down the stairs, bleeding but still alive when the attacker delivered the fatal shot to the back of his left ear.

The police then found his wallet with cash and credit cards still on his person. The scene now looked less like a robbery and more like a targeted execution. After recovering the shell casings (a 9mm pistol was the culprit) they went upstairs to Michelle's office. Inside, they discovered that Michelle had used the toilet (and didn't flush) as well as leaving an empty candy wrapper in the trash.

Police noted that it was almost as if she went upstairs to wait *something* out. If she were, in fact, looking for a book, it would not have taken that long.

The police released Michelle on her own recognizance. The next morning, they returned to the office and spoke to her employer, Dr. Harbin. The doctor would reveal that Michelle had been having marital trouble and was having an affair with John Diamond.

Police now saw John Diamond as the man with the motive. But when they interviewed Lourdes Diamond, John's wife, she said that she was home with her husband that entire evening, watching a movie. The police became discouraged.

Then Lourdes added that John got a call about 9 p.m. that evening and that he quickly left the house. She stated that John changed his clothes, put on parka clothing and told her that he had to go to the barracks.

Police then checked out the phone records on John's cell phone and noted that he did receive a call from Michelle.

Michelle would later deny that she ever called John that night.

After receiving the cell phone records, however, it became evident that John and Michelle had called each other twenty times a day at a minimum. They had exchanged a phone call about ninety minutes prior to Marty being shot to death.

When pressed on his involvement with Michelle, John admitted to the affair.

"She is one of many," John said. "She's a side piece. I have a lot of women."

Michelle would later claim that she conducted her own detective work after Marty's death. She stated that she went to John's home and asked him if he knew anything about the murder.

"I asked him 'do you know anything about this,'" Michelle said. "'Do you know anybody who had anything to do with this?' He said 'No, I would never do anything to hurt you. I know how much you loved him.' I believed him. He looked so trustful."

Police would dismiss Michelle's confrontation with John. They tailed him around town, watching him park in front of the Theer home and sneak inside through the back door.

John would remain there the whole night.

"He knew I was depressed," Michelle said. "And I was getting more and more depressed. I think I went to John for comfort."

John and Michelle would then travel to Florida as Marty's murder investigation was ongoing. The official reason according to Michelle:

Grief counseling.

She claimed there was a former professor there in the state that would be able to help her cope with Marty's death.

While in Florida, John went to live with his sister, Debbie Dvorak.

"He acted as if nothing was wrong," Dvorak said. "He knows he had nothing to do with it. He didn't shoot him."

The physical evidence remained weak. The police continued to sift through the cell phone records and came across the phone number of one of John's army friends. Calling him up, they asked if John would have access to any 9mm weaponry. The friend would reveal that he had, in fact, loaned out his gun to John. The transaction took place just days before Marty's murder. The Smith & Wesson Model 5906 that he loaned John would be the same type of weapon used to kill Marty. All the police had to do was obtain the murder weapon and they would have the physical evidence required to indict.

Then, as if on cue in a mystery movie, John Diamond reported a break-in of his car in the base parking lot.

"Did they steal anything?" a reporting officer asked.

"Yeah," John said. "My friend's gun. Jesus, he's going to be pissed."

But John made a mistake.

There was a pile of glass outside the car which would indicate that the passenger side door had been open during the "break-in". John had smashed the window himself and feared getting glass on the interior of his car.

The US Army investigators would charge John with obstruction of justice, conspiracy, and premeditated murder. The Army officials relayed their findings to civilian police and wanted them to charge Michelle. Five months later, John would be court-martialed. Michelle would be called as a witness but invoke her Fifth Amendment right with every question.

"John would have a cocky air about him throughout his trial," Orange said. "He joked with reporters and smiled at the jury. He felt certain that he would be acquitted."

His cocky demeanor would backfire. The jury would find John guilty and he was convicted of all counts. His current wife Lourdes would testify that John would receive a phone call in the evening and leave the home. His mother-in-law would also testify that he had come home in the middle of the night and began washing clothes.

John would be sentenced to life without parole.

But Michelle Theer remained free.

"What I got from him (John) after he was arrested was that he didn't want anything to do with her," his sister Debbie said. "Nothing. You don't expect to be convicted on theory. On myths. Show me blood. Show me a gun. Show me a time-line that works. Show me those facts. I'll believe until the day I die that she (Michelle) killed her husband, that she planned to have my brother go down for it, so she could live this happy, wonderful life."

"From my opinion, if he (John) wanted to shoot someone he could have shot someone from a mile away. Why sneak up on somebody and shoot them five times and even according to the coroner, they're all over the place. Whoever shot that weapon wasn't a sharp shooter. Didn't know how to shoot a weapon, was scared to be there, whatever, they were all over the place. Ricocheting off of this and ricocheting off of that. There's just no way."

Upon John's conviction, Michelle left town. She moved to New Orleans until the Fayetteville police finally got the grand jury to indict her on charges of first-degree murder in May of 2002.

Michelle fled the city, however, and became a fugitive on the run.

"I think she planned to kill her husband a long time ago," Dvorak said. "I think she waited and researched and waited for that right person who would look and fit the part to pin it on."

During John's trial, Michelle had begun her preparation. She purchased pamphlets such as REBORN IN THE USA, HOW TO DISAPPEAR IN AMERICA, and SECRETS FOR GETTING A NEW IDENTITY, obtaining tips on how to evade detection from authorities. Michelle also obtained a few books on learning Spanish and travel guides to several Latin countries like Mexico. She bleached her hair blonde and used a high-end printer to make both fake birth and baptismal certificates.

Michelle was dead serious about evading capture. Hiding out in Florida, she paid to have plastic surgery done on her nose, chin and had laser surgery to remove her acne and other skin blemishes.

From an appearance standpoint, she had fully reinvented herself. Michelle was able to fool the DMV and get a driver's license under the alias of "Alexandra Solomon." She rented an apartment under the name of "Lisa Pendragon" from Cynthia Geesey in Lauderdale by the Sea, Florida.

"She told me that she was on the run from an abusive boyfriend in California," Geesey said. "I thought she was well-spoken and articulate."

Geesey allowed Michelle to sign the six-month lease, believing her story. Michelle would blend into her surroundings rather easily. She made a few friends around the neighborhood and found a new boyfriend. She then called her parents from a pay phone in town to let them know she was okay.

"She was always a little apprehensive," Geesey said. "Always looking over her shoulder. That's the only thing I found a little strange about her. I was talking to her one day in front of her apartment and there was a helicopter overhead. And she freaked out! Ran back inside. I said 'It's just a helicopter' and she said 'I don't know, it might be my boyfriend.' And I found that a little odd. But other than that she seemed pretty reasonable , paid her rent on time. Took good care of her animals, no other problems with her."

Fayetteville police were at a loss in locating Michelle and enlisted the aid of United States Marshals. True to form, they knew that Michelle could not resist male companionship and caught a break. Michelle instructed her new boyfriend to call her parents from a pay phone in order to relay a message. Her new beau, however, made the mistake of calling Michelle's family from his parent's home. The U.S. Marshals were already tracing all of Michelle's calls and they quickly found out the identity of her new boyfriend.

Placing him under watch, Michelle's new beau soon led authorities straight to her.

After being on the run for three months, Michelle had been finally been captured.

THE AFTERMATH

Michelle's case took two years to go to trial. She would turn down a plea deal which would send her to prison for only ten years. The case then went to trial for ten weeks, drawing both local and national media attention.

Despite the lengthy trial, the jury returned after only six hours of deliberation.

Marty Theer's mother, Linda, waited in nervous anticipation as the verdict was read.

"Guilty."

Linda shook with emotion and tears as the word was spoken. For her, she felt relief that the trial was finally over.

"He (Marty) was a very, very tender person," Linda said. "There wasn't a mean bone in his body. He wouldn't have anything bad to say about anybody. I wish I could say the same."

Michelle would be sentenced to life in prison without the possibility of parole. She is currently housed at the North Carolina Correctional Institute for Women in Raleigh, North Carolina.

John is currently imprisoned at the United States Disciplinary Barracks at Fort Leavenworth, Kansas.

Both John and Michelle have made attempts to obtain a new trial without success.

THE BONDAGE MURDERS : THE TRUE STORY OF SHIRLEY WITHERS

MARY MAXWELL

Shirley Withers and Peter Shellard looked to be a mismatched couple.

Shellard was a multi-millionaire dollar real estate mogul and high-end car dealer. Logic would dictate that he would date much younger women, seducing aspiring actresses and models with his wealth. But Shirley was anything but a supermodel. She was an ordinary looking bookkeeper, thirty-three-years-old, and bit on the frumpy side.

"He was a hot shot," forensic psychologist Paula Orange said. "An eccentric hotshot but still very well-to-do. He would strut around town wearing fancy suits with matching socks but wear sandals over them. Shirley, on the other hand, was very unassuming. She looked like the typical cubicle drone. A little overweight and plain looking. Nothing sexy about her."

Their relationship, however, would be one of the biggest firestorms of sex, murder, and drugs in Australian history.

BEGINNINGS

Shirley was born in New Delhi, India in 1966. She immigrated with her family to Australia when she was a child. She married young and had two sons with her first husband. By 2000, she would be divorced and immediately be on the market for a new beau.

Enter Peter Shellard.

Peter, born in 1949, touted himself as a self-made millionaire although he had a benefactor in an older, maternal figure in Vera Moore.

He didn't finish high school, dropping out to obtain his real estate agent's license at night. Once he acquired that, he began leveraging properties around the Brighton area eventually making a fortune in addition to buying a high-end car dealership.

He called his company "Peter Shellard Real Estate" and then used that money to help finance a deal where he took control over Kellow-Falkiner Motors. He juggled both real estate as well as used Rolls-Royce and Bentley parts.

Shellard's businesses continued to flourish. He purchased many companies as well as commercial and rental properties.

"He hung around some heavy hitters in his area," Orange said. "People who could buy Rolls Royces without batting an eye."

Shellard would purchase the Rosecraddock Place in North Caulfield, a regal mansion which would later sell for over $7 million upon his death. As his wealth grew, he began collecting high-end cars which included a 1923 Rolls-Royce, a 1951 Rolls-Royce Silver Dawn, and a Mercedez-Benz 450SL convertible.

AN ECCENTRIC NUT

Shellard did have mental issues, however, suffering from bipolar disorder.

"His mansion was filled with all kinds of knick-knacks," Orange said. "Stuff that seemed disconnected and junky. But he was bipolar and people with that ailment tend to have different eccentricities. His was to hoard stuff among other things."

Shellard was reported to be a recluse, sheltering himself from the outside world as he became more wealthy. He had a barbed wire fence built high around the mansion but it served more to keep him in then keeping people out. His neighbors would rarely see him outside the compound unless he was walking his dogs. He also had ponies and kept an area for beehives. Neighbors complained about the bees and the city had the hives destroyed. Shellard would later file suit and demand that he have the remains of his dead bees returned.

Shellard would treat other homeowners as if they were peasants and would come and go on their private grounds as he pleased. One neighbor reported that Shellard came into their backyard and began sifting through their garden tools. Another complained that Shellard would park one of his Rolls-Royces in their personal garage. Shellard was informed to remove the vehicle after which he became enraged and began to tear apart the garage. He would then be sued for the action and was forced to pay almost $2000 in damages.

"Obviously, he walked around as if he had a sense of entitlement," Orange said. "Definitely a narcissistic sociopath but he could turn on the charm when he wanted. It all depended on what he wanted. When he was trying to make a sale, he could charm you. When he was doing something stupid and you called him on it, that is when he went berserk."

Town councilwoman Veronika Martens had plenty of bizarre dealings with Shellard as well. On one occasion, Shellard chopped down some cypress trees on his property and began burning the branches. Neighbors called to complain and firefighters came down to extinguish the flames.

Enraged, Shellard began attacking the firefighters and cut through the fire hoses with an ax.

Later, Shellard would be caught breaking into Caulfield Town Hall by climbing in through the roof. He would also come into the building unannounced, enter unoccupied offices and begin making phone calls.

"Shellard was an aggressive, anti-government guy," Orange said. "He went so far as to try to have his mansion designated as a religious place in order to avoid taxes. The judge got a good laugh at that one. The religion of what? Nutty behavior?"

Angered that his request was denied, he began making plans to tear down the mansion and divide up the land. But legal maneuverings blocked him from doing that as city council members had his mansion placed on the Historic Buildings Council, giving it legal protection.

A SADO-MASOCHIST

A ladies man, Shellard would marry twice. He had three daughters, Jenny, Clare and Sarah, before divorcing his second wife Elizabeth in 1994.

Shellard really did not have any bad habits that than his eccentricities as he abstained from both alcohol and smoking. He did have one fetish, however, and that was sadomasochism.

Shellard would go to clubs and participate in bondage sessions, preferring visits to the Hellfire Club in Brighton. Once there, he would "dress up in a full range of leather outfits and had belts with studs."

Shellard would go to the Hellfire Club to be whipped.

"He told me initially that his pain threshold was very low," Shellard's friend Christine Smith said. "And after a number of visits his tolerance for pain increased to the point where he really liked what was occurring. He found it very erotic."

By 2001, he was looking for a new partner and found one in Shirley Withers.

"Initially mum and I thought Shirley was a bit odd," Jenny, Shellard's eldest daughter recalled. "She would never look you in the eye. She was always very kind, though."

ENTER SHIRLEY WITHERS

Opposites attract, and Shellard soon began wooing Shirley with his luxurious lifestyle. He brought her numerous gifts, jewelry, and clothing.

"I'll bankroll all your dreams," he teased.

Shirley took him up on the offer, expressing her desire to run her own clothing boutique.

"Shellard did anything and everything for Shirley," forensic psychologist Paula Orange said. "He bought her everything she asked for evening financing her 'dream' of running a boutique store in a prestigious area of Brighton. Never mind the fact that Shirley had no business experience. Shellard believed he had money to burn."

"You can't be serious?" Shirley gushed when Peter told her he would buy her a clothing company.

"What are you going to call it?" Shellard asked, smiling.

"God," Shirley said. "God. I don't know. How about Suzette? Suzette Boutique?"

"Suzette Boutique!" Shellard laughed aloud as Shirley hugged him in appreciation.

Shellard made all the arrangements for Shirley to run the store. He had it designed and built to her specifications.

Shirley would have all of the brand name fashions in her store. She loaded the shelves with Marianna Hardwick, Charlie Brown, and Lisa Ho.

Shellard had one caveat and that was having his eldest daughter, Jenny, work in the boutique. Jenny herself, however, had a less than flattering impression of both Shirley and her attempts to run a business.

"My first impression when I started working there was that it was just a mess," Jenny said. "I couldn't understand how Shirley kept paying us every week. I had seen invoices totaling thousands of dollars and wondered where Shirley was getting the money. Shirley would just continuously buy stock for the business and for herself. She definitely had a problem with spending money."

Shellard did not stop at just buying Shirley her own boutique.

He bought her a house.

"It was a bit of an odd arrangement," Orange said. "They had separate living quarters. Shellard wanted his own house to himself and would visit Shirley for coital purposes."

Shellard displayed further bad judgment when he allowed Shirley to be put in charge of the accounting of his car dealership.

"He figured she was a bookkeeper," Orange said. "She must know what she's doing."

Shellard's naivete didn't end there as he allowed Shirley access to his property accounts in addition to becoming a signatory on his car dealership.

What Shellard didn't take into account was that Shirley was not a person he could trust nor did she know what she was doing.

Her boutique began to fail. She had purchased too much product and the few items that did sell would not have a high enough margin. Being a marginal business person, she continued to purchase inventory despite not generating any revenue.

The store began losing money. Lost of it.

So Shirley took it upon herself to begin stealing from Shellard's dealership. She would write checks to herself in upwards of $10,000. Shellard began noticing the discrepancies and called in his accountant.

After checking the books, the two realized that Shirley stole over $900,000, a significant amount of Shellard's wealth.

NO CURE FOR A SPENDAHOLIC

Shellard owned over eleven properties and his total net worth looked to be about $10-15 million.

By the time Shellard had finally got wind of Shirley's financial doings, she had amassed over $43,000 in credit card debt while her store was almost $275,000 in the red.

"She simply had no idea what she was doing," Orange said. "She spent and spent and spent."

To top it off, she had siphoned nearly a million dollars from the dealership account, funding the boutique and her own shopping sprees.

"She's robbing you blind," the accountant said. "You should go to the police."

"I'll take care of it," Shellard said. "Let me handle it."

Shellard began to take action. He informed his bank that he wanted Shirley removed as the signatory for his automotive dealership. Then he called a meeting with his friend, Eugene Hand and his lawyer Stuart Winston

"She's ripping me off," Shellard said. "The bitch is robbing me blind. She shuttled over $150,000 into her own account."

"You need to call the police," Winston said.

"I'm going to sell her house," Shellard said. "Fuck her. I need to recoup that loss."

Shellard then confronted Shirley about stealing his money. He was livid, demanding to know what she had been doing.

"He obviously felt betrayed," Orange said. "He was crazier than a shithouse rat, but let's face it, the guy had been good to her. He bought her everything she wanted and let her join him in this decadent lifestyle. But it wasn't good enough for her. She stole his credit cards. Wrote checks in his name payable to her."

Shirley didn't feel remorse at the dressing down by Shellard. She just didn't want the gravy train to leave.

THAT MONEY AIN'T GOING NOWHERE

Shirley began looking for a solution. She noticed a scraggly, down and out woman visiting her boutique often and a light bulb went on her head.

The woman was named Sophia.

Sensing she was a person with some wrong side of the street connections, Shirley saw Sophia and her boyfriend Stanley as "useful idiots" in a plot to kill her husband. They were low-level drug dealers willing to do anything for a buck.

Even if it included murder.

"Shirley gave them a song and dance about how she was an abused spouse," Orange said. "She told the two junkies that she had to endure nightly beatings and rapes. How Shellard would tie her up and have his way with her."

Sophia and Stanley, despite being heroin addicts and petty criminals, felt moral indignation.

Then Shirley waved a few thousand dollars in their face and they were willing to do whatever she asked.

On May 6th, 2005, Shirley lead the two junkies into Shellard's home.

"He's sound asleep in his bed until Shirley attacks him, placing a pillow case over his head," Orange said. "The two junkies hold Shellard down but he begins to fight. He struggles with Sophia and bites her finger. The junkie screams and takes some kind of heavy object from the bedside table and smashes Shellard over the head with it."

Shellard is knocked unconscious but that is when Shirley goes to work.

She takes a needle and injects him with heroin as she wants to make everything look like an overdose.

Then they pulled down his pants.

"Shellard is starting to come to," Orange said. "Then they shove a suppository up his rectum. Oxycontin. This coupled with the heroin is a powerful mix as he has a heart condition. A knock on the head, a shot of heroin and some Oxycontin shoved up his ass killed the man."

Peter is left for dead as Shirley lets some time pass before she calls the police.

A BAD ACTRESS AND A PAIR OF BUNGLING CRIMINALS

Shirley then conjures up her best Meryl Streep act as she calls the police and tells them that she has found Shellard dead on the floor.

"He was into rough sex," she blubbered. "I don't know who could have done this to him."

Police arrived and found the dead Shellard with a towel covering his genitals. His ankles were handcuffed and he was wearing a mouth gag. He also had dog leads, electrical cords and ropes tied around him.

Unfortunately for Shirley, however, the two junkies she hired were not exactly professionals.

A fingerprint sweep led police to Sophia.

Her print had been found on a hallway telephone. They would also find her DNA on a partially smoked cigarette in the kitchen.

The police would track down Sophia as well as her junkie boyfriend. They both confessed to the crime.

"I did it," Stanley said the moment he took a seat in the interrogation room. "Well, I should say that I helped them do it. Shirley drove me and Sophia to the mansion. She wanted him tied up because he had forced her to do bondage with him. Bondage! The dude had frozen all her accounts and was trying to sell her house behind her back. She told him that she wanted to sign some papers so that she could get her house back."

Stanley described the evening of the killing as a casual night on the town. He stated that Shirley took Sophia and himself to a hotel for some gambling.

"We played the poker machines," Stanley told the police. "Then we got some heroin and went to the mansion. Shirley had a syringe of heroin. She went into his bedroom and stuck him with it."

Shellard's daughters, all decent young women, were in shock at what happened to her father. Shirley took it upon herself to try and comfort Jenny but didn't mince words about the kind of man he was.

"Your father was into bondage," Shirley said to her after she tried to sell the police on the fact that Shellard's death was likely due to rough sex. "We never hurt each other, though."

"After my dad died, I confided in Shirley for support," Jenny said. "I thought that she would be the only one who could possibly understand the pain I was going through because she was going through it too."

Shirley didn't know that while she was talking daily on the phone with Jenny, the police had her phone tapped.

They would find out that Shirley was calling around asking for a hitman.

Setting up a sting, they assigned an undercover officer for the operation.

A HITMAN COMETH

Shirley made it known that she was looking for someone to "off" both Sophia and Stanley, thereby getting rid of her only witnesses.

An undercover officer, code-named "Victor" called Shirley and set up four meetings.

"Can you get me pictures of them?" Victor asked.

"No," Shirley said. "But I can get you their address."

"What do they do for a living?"

"They don't 'do' anything," Shirley scoffed. "They're fucking junkies. They sit around all day and shoot heroin."

"Why do you want them killed?"

"They were responsible for killing my husband," Shirley said. "I want them both taken care of."

"It will cost you ten thousand dollars," Victor said. "I need three grand up front. Down payment."

"No problem."

"I need you to get as specific as you can," the hitman said. "Do you want it to be quick or do you want them to suffer?"

"Yes," Shirley said, her eyes cold.

"But do you want them dead?" the hitman asked again. "Or in a wheelchair for the rest of their lives?"

"I want them both dead," Shirley said with finality. "Dead."

Shirley would be arrested and charged with Shellard's murder while the two junkies would receive six years in jail for manslaughter.

In 2007, however, Shirley would elect to go to trial. In her appeal, she somehow convinced the judge that she didn't mean to kill Shellard. She only meant to teach him a lesson.

Shirley would be sentenced to thirteen years in prison which could be lessened to nine years with good behavior.

At the time of this writing, Shirley has become eligible for parole.

A FINAL BETRAYAL

The story took another turn for the bizarre when trustees of Vera Moore's estate would claim that millions of dollars that Moore gave Shellard were meant as a loan and not a gift.

They argued that it should be repaid.

Moore had died eight years prior to Shellard being murdered. He had been a good friend of her son, Kenneth, who died in a car crash in 1972.

Moore then took a shine to the young Shellard, treating him as if he were her own son.

She would give him her son's Waring Bros Tourer Rolls-Royce. In return, Shellard would keep the elderly widow company. He would take her out of her suburban nursing home and drive her around in the Rolls-Royce while they would go out for tea.

"By all accounts," Orange said. "He seemed to have been good to her. Like a son. He was soon given the power of attorney for her and looked after her financial affairs."

Shellard would purchase the Rosecraddock mansion in 1984 for $1.4 million. This was done with Moore's money as the title was split between her company, Brenchley Gardens, and Shellard's company then called "Landro."

Shellard would always seem to have bad luck with women, not only while alive but in death as well as even the attorneys for his mother figure in Vera Moore would turn on him.

KATHERINE KNIGHT

CARL KEITH

Katherine Mary Knight was born to shed blood. Born October 24th, 1955, she has the distinction of being the first Australian woman to be sentenced to life without the possibility of parole when she murdered her de facto husband John Charles Thomas Price, born 6 January 1955, in Aberdeen, New South Wales, Australia. The murder itself is not necessarily the stuff of horror films or nightmares with extreme heinousness even though Knight did, in fact, stab Price 37 times. Knight's subsequent defilement of Price's body following the murder was extremely atrocious and, as such, was the fundamental reason she received a life without parole sentence. So heinous, in fact that her file is marked "never to be released."

After stabbing Price to death, Knight proceeded to utilize her career skills as a butcher in an abattoir (slaughterhouse) to expertly and precisely excise Price's skin from his corpse in one piece which she hung from a meat hook inside an archway of the house before decapitating him and boiling his head with some vegetables for dinner. She also cut pieces from the victim's buttocks and cooked those as well, making two dinner plates with vegetables for Price's children. As a result, Knight is often referred to among Australians as the "Black Knight" and Aberdeen—once a charming small community named for Aberdeen, Scotland, located approximately 266 kilometers north-northwest of Sydney with a population slightly less than 1,800 that was known for its picturesque countryside, abattoirs, and as the birthplace of the blue heeler cattle dog—is now permanently blemished by Katherine Knight and her heinous crime.

Early Life

Knight was born at Tenterfield Hospital in Aberdeen, New South Wales, Australia, to Barbara Roughan (nee Thorley) who already had four boys—Patrick, Martin, Neville, and Barry—from a prior marriage and another son, Charlie, with her current lover and Katherine's father Ken Knight, an abattoir slaughterman. Barbara was forced to move to another town following cultivating a relationship with Ken, one of her then-husband's co-workers. This relationship was a scandal because of both families' renown within the town. At the time, Jack Roughan had four children and while his two older ones stayed with him and Barbara, the two younger ones were sent to Sydney to live with an aunt. Barbara then gave birth to twins Katherine and Joy, with Joy a half an hour older than Katherine. When the twins were four, Jack died and his two older children moved in with the Knights.

Knight had a troubling upbringing, to say the least. Due to her maternal great-grandmother's Aboriginal heritage and the overwhelming racism in the area at that time, the resulting tension was difficult for all of the children. As a result, Knight was a relatively isolated child; the only people with whom she was close were her twin sister and her Uncle Oscar Knight who, tragically, committed suicide in 1969. Following this heartbreak, the Knights moved back to Aberdeen.

Compounding her isolation, Knight had to contend with an alcoholic father who resorted to intimidation and violence regularly. It is reported that Ken would sexually assault Barbara as many as ten times per day. Barbara shared intimate details of her sex life and her contempt for men and sex with both Katherine and Joy. Further—as if the aforementioned was not enough—Knight claimed repeated sexual abuse by several family members (not her father, though) until she was 11 years old. Despite psychiatrists believing that this did occur, specific details are in doubt. Nonetheless, it is generally widely-accepted that she did suffer said abuse.

Amidst all of this turmoil in her life, everyone who knew her as a child said that while Knight was a generally pleasant girl who earned recognition and awards for her good behavior she did experience uncontrollable rages in response to seemingly minor upsets. During her high school years at Muswellbrook High School she was remembered by former classmates as a bully who attacked at least one student with a weapon and also assaulted a teacher who, in self-defense, injured Knight.

Knight ultimately left school at 15, virtually illiterate. She was, however, able to obtain employment in a clothing factory as a fabric cutter. One year later, at the age of 18, she began working at the local abattoir where her job was to decapitate the pigs; something in which she took great interest and pleasure, often watching the pigs having their throats slit before they reached her. Whereas some of her coworkers thought her behavior to be rather macabre, they just chalked it up to her taking an interest in all aspects of her employer's function. Soon thereafter she secured what she called her "dream job" as an offal (animal organs) cutter at the abattoir. Not long after this Knight was promoted to boner and given her very own set of razor-sharp butcher knives; what she called her most prized possessions. Knight—at every place she ever lived—hung her knives on a nail above her bed so, according to her, they "would always be handy if [she] needed them."

When one, after the fact, examines Knight's early life there are many indications that she would have likely snapped and resorted to murder. If people would have not chalked her erratic behavior up to her "normal" state and reported her disturbing behavior perhaps much of her mayhem could have been prevented.

A Series of Failed Relationships

David Kellett

Knight met her first husband, 22-year old truck driver and hard-drinking David Stanford Kellett in 1973 and as soon as Knight turned 18 she moved in with him. The relationship was one where Knight wore the proverbial pants. If Kellett got into a fight due to his drinking, Knight would be there to use her fists, if necessary, to back him up. In fact, throughout Aberdeen Knight was known for "offering armed combat to anyone who upset her."

Despite her domination of him, Kellett agreed to marry Knight in 1974—at her request. Her mother told Kellett on their wedding day that he had better watch Knight "or she'll fuc*ing kill you." She warned him that if he said or did the wrong thing, cheated on her, or otherwise stirred her up that Knight would not hesitate to kill him. Barbara also told Kellett that her daughter had "a screw loose somewhere." He didn't have to wait long to find this out for himself. On their wedding night after Kellett fell asleep after having sex with Knight only three times, she tried to strangle him for failing to perform to her expectations.

Things progressed from bad to worse with a pregnant Knight burning all of Kellett's clothing and shoes before assaulting him with a frying pan to the back of his head after he came home late from a darts competition at a local pub. Kellett sustained a fractured skull from the altercation and while he initially wanted to press charges against her, Knight—in her loving, best behavior—got him to change his mind. In fact, Kellett was so afraid of his wife that he secretly sought medical care the following day at work.

In May 1976 Knight gave birth to the couple's first child; a daughter named Melissa Ann. Shortly thereafter Kellett tired of Knight's possessiveness and domineering, violent behavior and left her for another woman. The pair fled to Queensland which, as would be expected, did not sit well with his wife. The next day, Knight was seen violently pushing Melissa in a pram down the main street, shaking it roughly from side to side and also stole an axe from a neighbor's back yard and swung it about her head threatening to kill random people. Subsequently, Knight was admitted into St. Elmo's Hospital in Tamworth where she received a diagnosis of postpartum depression. She remained in the hospital for several weeks. Shortly after her release, she left two-month old Melissa on railway tracks soon before a train was expected to arrive. If it wasn't for a homeless man who was known around town as "Old Ted" foraging near the tracks and who heard Melissa crying, the baby would have been killed. Arrested for her negligence, Knight was sent back to St. Elmo's but signed herself out the following day.

Within a week Knight cut the face of local teenager 16-year old Margaret Macbeth with one of her precious knives and ordered the woman to drive her to Queensland to find Kellett. Macbeth escaped when they stopped at a service station and by the time police arrived Knight was threatening a small boy she had taken hostage with her knife. Police disarmed her by attacking her with brooms and she was subsequently admitted into the Morisset Psychiatric Hospital where she told anyone who would listen to her how she was frequently abused by Kellett. She also informed the nurses that she was planning to kill the service station mechanic because he had fixed Kellett's car which then allowed him to leave with his new girlfriend. Knight added that she had planned to murder both Kellett and his mother when she reached Queensland.

After finding out about his wife's plans and disturbing behavior Kellett left his new girlfriend and he and his mother moved to Aberdeen to take care of Knight who was released on 9 August 1976 into their care. Knight, Kellett, and Kellett's mother subsequently moved to Woodridge, a suburb of Brisbane, where Knight was overjoyed to find work at the Dinmore Meatworks in nearby Ipswich.

Shortly thereafter, another example of her ability to attack without provocation involved a local police officer who Knight stabbed but—as was the case with every prior assault—she was never charged. Kellett also recounted another incident wherein he awakened one morning to find Knight straddling his chest grazing his throat with one of her knives. He said that she just laughed at him and stated how easy it would have been for her to kill him. An informative omen, to say the least.

Despite all of the disturbing behavior Knight displayed, Kellett got her pregnant again and on 6 March 1980 little Natasha Maree was born; however, in 1984 the marriage completely disintegrated due to Knight's constant jealousy of Kellett's truck driving job and relentless allegations of his having girlfriends everywhere and she ultimately left him, moving in with her parents back in Aberdeen for a short while before renting a house on McQueen Street in nearby Muswellbrook where she returned to her prior job at the abattoir. Kellett learned of this by returning home from work one night to an empty house.

In 1985, Knight injured her back and was subsequently placed on disability where she received a disability pension. Soon thereafter, Knight again moved back to Aberdeen where she and her daughters lived in a Housing Commission house.

David Saunders

In 1986, Knight met 38-year old divorced miner David Saunders who, a few months after that, moved in with Knight and her daughters while simultaneously maintaining his own apartment in Scone. Saunders was smitten with Knight even knowing full well that she had several "shortcomings" such as attacking people with kitchen appliances, knives, and her fists, but he could not overlook the fact that she was cheerful and charming and possessed a voracious sexual appetite. As would be expected, Knight was extremely jealous about why he kept his apartment and accused him repeatedly of cheating on her. Knight repeatedly threw Saunders out of the house and he returned to Scone each time. Invariably she would seek him out and beg him to come back, which he did.

In May 1987 Knight slit the throat of Saunders' two-month old dingo puppy in front of him as an example of what she would do to him if he ever cheated on her. She then hit Saunders in the head with a frying pan, knocking him unconscious.

Not unlike Kellett, despite all of Knight's violence and unpredictability, in June of the following year, Knight gave birth to Saunders' and her daughter Sarah. Saunders put a deposit on a house that Knight paid off in 1989 with her workers' compensation settlement. Disturbingly, Knight heavily decorated the family house with animal pelts, skulls, leather jackets and old boots, machetes, rusty animal traps, horns, rakes, and pitchforks. And as usual, her butchering knives were hung on the wall above the de facto marital bed.

Another altercation between Knight and Saunders occurred that resulted in Knight hitting Saunders in the face with an iron prior to stabbing him in the stomach with scissors. Of course, he moved back to his Scone apartment during which time Knight had cut up all of his clothes; something he discovered upon his return. She also vandalized his car and attempted suicide by overdosing on sleeping pills which led to her being admitted into yet another psychiatric hospital. This was the last straw and, subsequently, Saunders took a long leave of absence from work and went into hiding. Knight tried to find him but nobody admitted to her whether or not he or she knew where Saunders was. When he tried to return to visit his daughter, Knight had already reported to the police that she was afraid of him and was issued an Apprehended Violence Order (AVO)—similar to a restraining order in the United States—against him.

John Chillingworth

In 1990, Knight became pregnant by 43-year old abattoir worker—and her former coworker—John Chillingworth. In 1991 she gave birth to a boy named Eric. Not surprisingly, from the beginning of their relationship volatility ensued. Chillingworth, a recovering alcoholic, did admit that he struck Knight once after she had pushed him too far after hitting him in the face, knocking his glasses off his face and breaking his dentures in his mouth. Their relationship lasted three more years before she left him for yet another man; a man with whom she had been having an affair for some time: John Price.

John Price

John "Pricey" Price already had three children when he met and began an affair with Knight. He was very well-liked and everyone who knew him described him as a "terrific bloke" whose own marriage ended in 1988. He had custody of his two older children while their then-two-year old daughter went to live with his ex-wife. Even though

Price was well aware of Knight's volatile reputation he still began an affair with her and in 1995 she and her children moved into his house. As was the case with all of her relationships, Price's and hers started out great; he had a steady, well-paying job in the local mines and her children liked him. However, their violent arguments—often precipitated by excessive alcohol consumption—intensified.

In 1998, Knight and Price argued because he refused to marry her so, in true retaliatory Katherine Knight form, she exacted revenge by videotaping items he had allegedly stolen from work and subsequently sending the tape to his boss. Even though the items consisted of out-of-date first aid kits that he found in the company's trash dumpster, Price was fired from the job he had worked for 17 years. Logically, Price kicked Knight out of his house and as she moved back to her own house the news of her actions quickly spread throughout the sleepy town.

Not unlike Knight's former lovers, Price couldn't stay away from her. Despite her horrible temper and violent streak, when she was loving and kind she was the perfect partner. Even though they restarted their relationship he refused to permit her to move back into his house. Of course, the fighting intensified because Knight did not have complete control over him. Additionally, because of his choice to continue to be with her Price lost many of his friends and acquaintances who refused to have anything to do with him while they were together.

In February 2000, Knight's assaults on Price increased, culminating with her stabbing him in the chest. Again, he kicked her out of his house and on 29 February he stopped by the Scone Magistrate Court on his way to work and took out an AVO on Knight—actually after discussing his fears with Knight's first husband, David Kellett—to keep her away from both him and his children. Price was able to secure new employment with Bowditch and Partners Earth Moving and was promoted to supervisor after 12 months and told his boss and coworkers that afternoon that if he failed to come to work the next day to expect that Knight had killed him. Despite his coworkers and boss urging him to not go back to her—even offering to let him stay with them—his worry for his children made him decline their gracious invitations. This would be the worst decision of his life.

When Price arrived home, his children were gone as Knight sent them to a friend's house for a sleepover. He spent a relaxing evening with the neighbors before retiring for the night at approximately 11:00 p.m. Knight arrived at Price's house later that night with the brand new black lingerie she had purchased earlier that day. Also earlier that day, Knight had videotaped herself singing nursery rhymes and hugging and kissing her children while making strange comments; the tape would later be referred to as some type of crude will in which she talked about hoping to be able to see them again. At Price's house, Knight watched television, took a shower, and climbed into his bed where she awakened him and the two of them had sex. Price fell back asleep afterward.

The Crime

Price was awakened by the first of 37 stab wounds Knight inflicted upon him with one of her prized, razor-sharp butcher knives. According to autopsy results, many of the wounds punctured vital organs. Blood evidence at the scene demonstrates that Price did, in fact, attempt to escape from Knight's attack and he actually managed to get to the front door—being repeatedly stabbed the entire time—before he was dragged back into the hallway where he finally exsanguinated and perished.

As if the brutal murder was not enough, what Knight did after Price died was extremely heinous and unbelievable.

After Price was dead, Knight skinned his body and hung the pelt—completely intact—from a meat hook through the head above an archway in his house. Interestingly, she left a small, one-inch square of skin intact upon his body that contained a scar from where she had previously stabbed him. Knight's skinning of Price's skin was so expertly done that following his autopsy, it was able to be reattached to his body in a manner indicative of a clear and appropriate methodology; thus underscoring Knight's adeptness due to her years of experience in the abattoir, likely coupled with her macabre fascination with knives, death, and similar topics.

She then decapitated him and placed his skinned head in a big stock pot on the stove with vegetables. The pot was still warm when police arrived the following morning. Knight also cooked parts of Price—later identified as his buttocks—and served them up as "steak" on two plates with zucchini, squash, cabbage, pumpkin, potatoes, and gravy atop the dinner table. Each plate had beside it a spiteful note for each of Price's children. Knight, apparently, was going to serve the children their own father for dinner. Another "meal" was found in the back yard with some speculating that it was for the dog and others conjecturing that Knight intended to consume parts of her lover but could not bring herself to eat it and discarded it.

She then returned to Price's headless and skinless corpse and arranged his body on the floor with his left arm resting atop an empty 1.25-liter Shelley's Club Lemon Squash soft drink bottle, his legs crossed, and a blood-stained, 31-centimeter yellow plastic-handled knife that matched the type of knife used to commit the heinous act by his right hand.

She also left a handwritten, blood-stained and flesh-covered note atop a picture of Price that read, "*Time you got back Johnathon for rapping [raping] my douter [daughter]. You to Beck [Price's daughter] for Ross—for Little John [Price's son]. Now play with little Johns Dick John Price.*" [sic] What Knight hoped to accomplish by penning this note is unknown and all of the accusations were proven to be baseless.

Knight has repeatedly claimed that she has no memory of what happened that fateful night after she and Price had sex.

Price's neighbor became concerned that his work vehicle was still in his driveway at 6:00 a.m. the following morning. Similarly, Price's employer was worried when he failed to arrive at work and sent a coworker to check on him. When the two men saw blood on the front door they called the police who arrived at Price's house at approximately 8:00 a.m. When police entered the house they were met with a grisly crime scene and discovered Knight on the bed comatose from attempting suicide with sleeping pills. After she had killed him, Knight drove to an Aberdeen ATM and withdrew $1,000 from Price's account and then swallowed the pills.

The police officers who found the macabre crime scene at 84 Andrews Street in Aberdeen testified that Knight had skinned Price so methodically that his entire skin—including face, ears, scalp, neck, and even his genitals—was completely intact and resembled that of a "macabre suit" only someone with her abattoir knowledge could achieve. Detective Senior Constable Peter Anthony Muscio issued the complete report that detailed the condition of Price's body, the tremendous amount of blood spatter and pooling throughout the house which indicated that Price did, in fact, fight vehemently for his life, and the gruesome discovery in the kitchen.

The crime scene was so disturbing, so utterly distressing, that many experienced police officers and forensic personnel assigned to the crime scene took stress leave soon after the investigation was completed. Some even admit to still suffering from elements of posttraumatic stress disorder suffered as a result. Even Knight's first husband, Kellett, admitted that he cried for days thinking about what she did and this was compounded by the fact that he had met and spoken to Price shortly before his demise. Kellett still fears for his life even though Knight will never be free again.

The Trial

Knight initially offered to plead guilty to manslaughter and, rightfully, was rejected. She was arraigned on 2 February 2001 for murder to which she pled not guilty. The trial was originally to commence on 23 July 2001 but was later reset for 15 October 2001 due to her attorney's illness. When the trial began, Justice Barry O'Keefe offered to excuse any of the 60 potential jurors who so desired due to the extremely graphic and disturbing photographic evidence that would be brought up during the trial. Five accepted. Several more asked to be excused when the witness list was revealed. Judge O'Keefe adjourned the trial after being informed that Knight wanted to change her plea to guilty and ordered a psychiatric evaluation that night to determine whether Knight understood the ramifications of a guilty plea and was legally sane to do so. Whereas Knight's attorneys initially planned to offer a defense of amnesia and dissociation—which the majority of psychiatrists supported—she was found to be legally sane despite what some psychiatrists thought to be the dominance of her primitive conscience; one that was ruled by the violence, incest, pedophilia, and rape that permeated her childhood. Knight had experienced more sex and violence than love throughout her life and the former dominated her relationships with others, particularly men. The speculation surrounding this proposed defense strategy was that Knight attempted to eat part of Price but the abhorrence she experienced caused her to dissociate from reality and to block everything out of her memory.

The next morning Knight changed her plea to guilty and the empaneled jury was dismissed. As there was no reason given why Knight changed her plea, it was speculated that when confronted with the horror of what she did when shown the crime scene photographs she wanted to spare jurors the similar horror of having to hear all of the gruesome details.

There is much comment in the literature that those who saw Knight sitting at the defense table admitted that she did not look like the vindictive monster that she truly was. It was well-known that she was not someone to cross and ex-lovers and family members testified at her trial that Knight was someone fully capable of considerable violence, even though when not in a murderous rage Knight was the perfect mother and housewife. Chillingworth testified about the incident where Knight killed his puppy and the story of how she got Price fired over an alleged stolen first aid kit was also introduced. Once all of the witnesses were finished testifying the general consensus was that her looks were not to be taken as fact and that someone far more dangerous lurked beneath her seemingly calm exterior. Knight's over-the-top mental and physical vindictiveness demonstrated—to many experts—her vehement belief in revenge and an overdeveloped sense of entitlement. She was also described as one who delighted in making people afraid of her and that she was incapable of true love and empathy as she did not receive either as a developing child. Additional speculation suggested that Knight had fantasized about killing a human being for years and when she did, took considerable pride in her "work"—her ultimate "triumph."

Once Price went to see the police to obtain an AVO against Knight, prosecutors argued that at this moment she put her murderous plot into motion as evidenced by purchasing new lingerie to wear while she seduced him, ensuring that her knives were sharp enough, and making sure that she had the right pots handy for his head. Psychiatrists and criminal profilers asserted that she derived great pleasure from the planning and her subsequent action.

At her trial, one of Australia's foremost criminal psychologists, Dr. Rod Milton, presented his findings following Knight's interview and asserted that she suffered from borderline personality disorder. Borderline personality disorder is a serious mental illness responsible for mood instability, unstable behavior, and typically stormy relationships. It usually affects more women and begins during adolescence or early adulthood. Those who suffer from the disorder commonly have serious problems regulating thoughts and emotions, act impulsively and oftentimes recklessly, and experience very unstable relationships—all of these traits occurred in droves with Knight. Additional symptoms prevalent in individuals with borderline personality disorder include fear of abandonment; an unstable self-image or confused self-identity; self-damaging behaviors such as excessive spending, promiscuity, substance abuse, reckless driving, or binge eating; self-injury or suicidal behavior or ideations; very random and often violent mood swings; a constant feeling of sadness or worthlessness; anger problems to include frequent loss of temper and/or physical altercations; and paranoia or loss of contact with reality. Those who knew Knight would likely say that she possessed virtually every single one of these qualities. Her extreme fear of abandonment led to her volatile temper and resultant physically violent behavior with her lovers, she attempted suicide on several occasions, her mood swings were frequent and severe, she was very promiscuous which led to her affairs and constant attempts to seduce lovers who had kicked her out, and she regularly consumed a considerable amount of alcohol. Experts link extreme fear of abandonment to the release of adrenaline and norepinephrine which likely account for the trademark severe mood swings and angry outbursts and Knight's continual fear of abandonment and accusations that her lovers were cheating on her resulted in an inordinate amount of these neurotransmitters coursing through her body.

Borderline personality disorder is believed to be an illness with both biological and environmental influences. Heredity and childhood abuse—particularly sexual abuse—have been theorized to be among the strongest predictors of whether someone has a greater predisposition to developing the disorder. Further, the brains of those with borderline personality disorder demonstrate structural abnormalities and resulting malfunction which suggests that the illness has a biological foundation. More specifically, those areas of the brain responsible for emotions and feelings demonstrate higher than average brain activity.

The name borderline personality disorder was originally so named as sufferers were considered to be on the "borderline" between neurosis and psychosis with some professionals asserting that the name was inaccurate. With respect to Knight, that she has frequently been called psychotic may demonstrate some validity in this moniker. The fundamental differences between neuroses and psychoses are that while the former are mild mental disorders, the latter result from gross mental and emotional disruptions to include personality changes; lost or changed contact with reality; projection of certain thoughts upon others; loss of the ego to the id; disorganized, bizarre, and irrational thought processes; and frequent hospitalization due to attempted suicide and/or other self-harming behaviors. Whereas the literature suggests that individuals with borderline personality disorder experience some alleviation of their impulsivity and volatility when they reach their 40's, such was not the case with Knight.

Another speculation regarding Knight's psychological nature involves piquerism, defined as sexual arousal by cutting or stabbing another's skin, sometimes resulting in death. The literature defines piquerism as a form of paraphilic sadism which can range from a single prick, to multiple stab wounds to an eroticized area, to elaborate cutting, stabbing, or mutilation; with the last eerily similar to Knight's treatment of Price's deceased body. Piquerism is closely associated with so-called "lust murders" in which the offender stabs or mutilates the victim. Other common attributes associated with piquerism include posing or propping of the deceased's body, inserting items into various bodily cavities, anthropophagy (eating flesh or consuming blood), and necrophilia. Knight did, in fact, pose Price's corpse and planned to feed his flesh to his children and, perhaps, attempted to consume some herself. Prevalence of this disorder is currently unknown.

Sentencing

At her sentencing hearing on 9 November 2001, despite having pled guilty, Knight never accepted responsibility for her actions in Price's death. At this hearing, Knight's legal team requested her removal from the courtroom so she wouldn't have to listen to all of the details that she had allegedly forgotten which was adamantly denied and she was given the harshest sentence allowed under Australian law. When Dr. Timothy Lyons—the medical examiner who conducted Price's autopsy—took the stand and described every single gory detail, Knight became hysterical and required sedation.

According to Dr. Lyons, Price, thankfully, was already dead when he was skinned. The skinning was conducted professionally with the razor sharp knife inserted beneath his collarbone and sliced across to the other shoulder before being cut down Price's chest, over his stomach to his pubic area where a "T" was cut so the knife sliced down the front of his legs to his feet before moving the knife back up his body, skinning the back of his arms and the top of his head before peeling the victim's skin off in one piece, exposing his intestines. The skin displayed every single one of Knight's 37 stab wounds. Price's head was then removed with a clean cut at the C3-C4 juncture just above his shoulders. Dr. Lyons stated that the entire process would have taking approximately 40 minutes. Further, Dr. Lyons testified that the myriad wounds entered Price's aorta, both of his lungs, his liver, his stomach, his pancreas, his colon, and left kidney that had part of it completely sliced off.

Just prior to handing down Knight's sentence, Justice O'Keefe said of Price that *"The last minutes of his life must have been a time of abject terror for him as they were a time of utter enjoyment for her...she has not expressed any contrition or remorse and if released she poses a serious threat to the security of society."* Knight was given a life sentence without the possibility of parole and became the first woman in Australia's history with the distinction of having her file marked "never to be released." Of particular interest was that Australia had no statutory prohibition to the defilement Knight committed against Price's corpse which precluded her being charged with additional crimes. Her actions were so out of the scope of the law that it was likely unbelievable that someone could do something like this to another human being.

Evidence of her premeditation was further indicated when she said to one of Price's daughters "I told him if he took me back this time it was to the death."

Post-Conviction

In June 2006, Knight appealed her life sentence, asserting that life without the possibility of parole was too severe for murder; however a three-judge panel in the New South Wales Court of Criminal Appeal consisting of Justices Peter McClellan, Megan Latham, and Michael Adams dismissed her petition in September of that same year citing that her crime was so appalling and "almost beyond contemplation in a civilized society." Justice McClellan stated during her appeal that "*The psychiatric evidence indicates that her personality is unlikely to change in the future and, if released, she would be likely to inflict serious injury or perhaps death on others.*"

It has been alleged that Knight was inspired the horror film *Resurrection* (1999) in which a serial killer tried to reconstruct the body of Christ with parts of his victims. There is some speculation that Knight was a copycat of sorts of a gruesome scene in which a body was killed, decapitated, and then skinned and hung on a meat hook.

BLUE EYED BUTCHER : THE TRUE STORY OF SUSAN WRIGHT

123

ASHLEY GORMAN

The murder of Jeff Wright was one of the most brutal and controversial in Texas history. His wife, Susan Wright, stabbed him in excess of 193 times before burying his body in a shallow grave in the back of their home. What followed was a media frenzy as Susan was dubbed as the "Blue Eyed Butcher." Court TV televised the entire trial while numerous media outlets devoted special segments to the case.

But the picture didn't fit.

Susan was depicted as this cold-blooded, sadistic killer. Everyone who has met her, however, has come away feeling that she was a shy, polite woman who could not harm a fly. The prosecuting attorney would claim that her politeness was just an act...Was it an act? Or did Susan simply snap after being abused one time too many?

EARLY LIFE

There were three of the children altogether, Susan, Cindy and a brother named Jim. They were raised in an upper-middle-class home in Harris County. Susan's mother was a stay at home mom while her father was a mechanical engineer.

A shy and reserved child, Susan stated that she walked on eggshells at home as her father would abuse her mother.

"She was trained to put on a smile and make everything seem like it was all right," forensic psychologist Paula Orange said. "It became normal for her to see a father yelling at her mother and she thought it was something that went on in every household."

Susan's sister, Cindy, would maintain that Susan would have trouble standing up for herself. She tried out for the drill team and was berated by one of the older girls. Susan felt so violated that she transferred to another school.

Susan was a mediocre student in high school and made C's in the majority of her classes. She didn't date much but tried to get attention from boys. She had one boyfriend tell her she was "too fat" which prompted Susan to lose almost twenty pounds. At the age of eighteen, she had a boyfriend that told her to work as a topless dancer at a strip club called the Gold Cup.

She worked as a stripper there for about two months but grew tired of it, stating that the money wasn't worth it and that she did it to feel better about herself.

Susan then used the money to go a local community college where she enrolled in a nursing program. Still needing extra cash, she found began working as a hair stylist. She dropped out the nursing program just as fast as she quit exotic dancing, stating that the curriculum was too time-consuming and would cost too much.

"There are two ways to look at Susan's early life," Orange said. "One is to say that she was into the cocaine and fast lifestyle that the stripper scene would provide. The other is to say that perhaps she was looking for acceptance. Being a topless dancer is going to be judged harshly by adults. But to the young men she was trying to get attention from, it would be seen as something pretty cool."

Jeff Wright would see that something "pretty cool" in Susan the moment he laid eyes on her at a get together on Galveston Beach in Texas.

THE HANDSOME SUITOR

Jeff had been a notorious party animal in school. He enjoyed booze and cocaine but began thinking more about settling down as he turned thirty.

He then met the twenty-one-year-old Susan at the beach. She was a struggling waitress, he was a successful carpet and tile salesman. Smitten by her pretty face and blonde hair, he began pursuing her with vigor, showering Susan with expensive gifts and fancy dinners.

After a few months of dating, Susan announced that she was pregnant. Jeff would tell her that it would be "okay" if she got an abortion but they decided to keep the baby and marry instead. Susan, however, was upset that Jeff waited until she was eight months pregnant to propose.

A week after his proposal, the young couple exchanged vows in a small ceremony near Houston, Texas.

Susan would later claim that Jeffrey would change dramatically after the wedding night. He would taunt Susan, calling her a "fat ass" as she gained weight during the pregnancy. Susan became depressed after the baby was born and Jeff mocked her even further for seeing a doctor who diagnosed her with postpartum depression.

Jeff's controlling behavior got worse with time. He disallowed Susan to take the anti-depressants the doctor had prescribed her. He then began limiting the people she could have in her life, allowing Susan to see her mother but she could only be out of the house for an hour and a half. Susan wanted to take classes at a junior college but Jeff did not allow it. He then became infuriated when Susan went to the campus to enroll anyway, signing up for an Internet course. She had been gone out of the house too long, however, and Jeff became enraged.

"You nasty whore," he screamed as she entered the home. "Are you cheating on me?"

Jeff would smoke marijuana just about every day but according to Susan, the cannabis never took the edge off his personality. She found him to always be easily irritated as anything could set him off. He would complain about problems at work and the utility bills being too high. Then he would single out Susan for keeping a dirty house, fixing a lousy meal or not allowing the kids run around the house screaming.

APPEARANCES CAN BE DECEIVING

On the surface, both Jeff and Susan put on a false front that their home was a place of domestic bliss.

The couple purchased a home in the White Oaks subdivision in the Cypress-Fairbanks area of Houston. This was a fairly affluent area and Jeff was still doing well financially selling carpets and tiles. Another child followed, a daughter they named Kailey, and Susan kept house like a modern day June Cleaver. She entertained friends, family, and neighbors with parties and made sure that her home was the tidiest on the block. Susan had a level of perfectionism which she applied to her home life, she cooked and cleaned, making sure dinner was made and served at the exact same time each day.

Susan also tended the garden and flowers outside the home while Jeff dug out the porch and was in the process of installing a fountain.

Domestic life didn't sit well with Jeff. The cocaine addiction soon got the best of him.

"There were rumors about Jeff," forensic psychologist Paula Orange said. "That he would go to strip clubs and have threesomes with strippers."

Susan knew when Jeff was going on a binge as would become hyperactive, getting too rough with both her and the children. Susan would state that Jeff had kicked, punched and slapped her around during his cocaine-fueled episodes.

"This needs to stop," Susan said as Jeff bounced off the walls in rage.

"You don't fucking tell me what to do," Jeff said, his eyes bleary red. "I'm a grown ass man and you don't give me the rules. I make the fucking rules."

Susan ran to her room.

NO WAY OUT

In the summer of 1999, Jeff had physically beat Susan one night. Susan waited for him to leave the next morning then she packed her bags and took her children to her sister's home. Jeff called her later and told her that a delivery truck was coming by.

"Pack all your stuff back in there," Jeff hissed. "Because if you don't, I will kill you or Bradley."

Fearing for her life, Susan complied.

Jeff's aggression may have been fueled by his cocaine addiction which got the family into financial debt. He also began dating other women.

"He would go through an Internet dating site," Orange said. "He gave Susan herpes. She confronted him about it and he told her that if she 'was a better wife he wouldn't need other women.'"

The belittling and beatings became a daily occurrence as time wore on but Susan never called the police.

"That was a bit problem for the defense during her trial," Orange said. "There were so few people who saw the abuse take place. She had a neighbor who reported that Susan looked terrified of Jeff at times and another who said she saw Jeff grab her by the arm once. But there was never a police report of any kind of domestic disturbance."

Susan would later state that she did not believe in divorce because of her Christian beliefs and that she didn't want to embarrass her family.

But by September of 2002, the marriage was in shambles. Jeff had a new job and wasn't making as much money as before. His cocaine and alcohol addiction had gotten worse. On one occasion, he came home drunk and urinated on their daughter's bed. He then bought an air rifle and hit Susan with the butt of the gun. On New Year's day 2003, his first words to his wife to start off the new year were "Happy fucking New Year, bitch. That will be your last."

THE FINAL STRAW

On the night of January 13th, 2003, Jeff went on another cocaine binge. He then began rough-housing with Bradley, trying to show his young son some boxing moves he learned at the local gym. The horseplay got out of hand as Jeff hit Bradley hard in the face. The boy began to cry and Jeff panicked, fearing Susan would hear.

He waited, fully expecting Susan to come in and investigate.

Minutes passed, then Jeff settled down and laid on the couch, luxuriating in the final hours of his cocaine high.

Susan then came in and took the children to bed. Jeff watched a little television and looked to doze off as the cocaine comedown began.

But his spirits were perked up again when Susan entered the living room wearing nothing more than a silk bathrobe. The light behind her illuminated her curves.

Jeff looked at his young wife with his mouth open. He reached over for the remote and turned off the television, following her into the bedroom without saying a word.

"Susan had enough," Orange said. "She was powerless against the two-hundred twenty pound Jeff in a fight. So she used the one thing that she knew Jeff could not refuse. The one area in their life that she had the power. Sex."

Jeff couldn't help but smile when he entered the bedroom. Susan had gone for an all-out seduction.

Susan looked up at Jeff and smirked as she began lighting red candles around the room. He could not take his eyes off his younger wife as she reached over and pressed play on the CD.

Slow and sexy music filled the air. No words were needed.

Jeff gulped hard. The pleasure of the cocaine buzz and the anticipation of his wife's hot body against his was more than he could bear. Jeff let Susan take the lead in his drug haze and he soon found himself with his back on the bed, buck naked.

Taking a pair of his neck ties, Susan began tying Jeff's arms to the headboard.

"What are you doing, baby?" he asked.

"Shhhh," she whispered as she moved down to his ankles and tied them to the footboard.

Tied down and spread-eagled on the bed, Jeff watched as Susan took one of the candles off the table.

Then she poured the hot wax on his upper thigh.

"The fuck you doing!"

Then she poured the melting wax over his testicles.

"Yaaarrrrgh!" Jeff screamed. "What the fuck!"

He writhed against the knots around his wrists. Susan had done a good job tying him down.

The room was now dimly lit as only a few candle lights remained. Jeff squinted in the darkness as Susan straddled him.

She held up a knife.

"What are you doing!!"

Jeff struggled against the knots again. Susan had done a good job of tying him up. She was a perfectionist.

She did a damn good job.

Jeff felt her take his penis in her hand, pressing the point of the blade against it with the other.

"The hell are you doing?" he screamed, his heart beating out of his chest.

"I've been way too nice to you," Susan said with calm authority. "I played the role of the meek housewife. I let you do what you want. Let you say whatever you want to me. But now, I'm tired. And it's time to turn the tables."

Susan nicked the blade across Jeff's penis.

Screams filled the air.

Susan then placed the point of the blade into his scrotum.

Jeff writhed and pulled against the knots. He could not free himself from the restraints around his wrists and ankles.

Susan then mounted him again and he saw the fiery evil in her eyes.

"Susan," he pleaded. "Please don't."

She stabbed Jeff in the eye first. Then his face and neck.

"She absolutely hated the man," Orange said. "She wanted to completely obliterate his face. It was an act of destruction where she completely wanted to remove his face."

Jeff screamed in pain. Susan began crying and screaming herself, a mixture of a battle cry and years of abuse breaking free. She screamed at Jeff, telling him about every wrong and act of abuse he threw her way.

Susan shrieked as she blitzed Jeff's body with the blade.

Jeff yelped in pain.

All the yelling, however, awoke Bradley.

He knocked on the door.

Susan quickly put on her bathrobe and walked the little boy back to his room.

"Why was daddy screaming?"

"Mommy and daddy are playing a game," Susan said. "Now you get some sleep."

After tucking Bradley back into bed, Susan went back to the bedroom.

Jeff, bloodied from over fifty knife wounds, was still alive.

"None of his wounds," Orange said. "Would have been enough to kill Jeff on its own. So he was laying there in excruciating pain, bleeding out.

Susan then got a second knife from the kitchen, a butcher knife. She returned to the bedroom and resumed her attack, stabbing Jeff another 140 times. The majority were to his face and neck but she attacked his genitals as well.

Tired from the stabbing, Susan caught her breath, waiting for the adrenaline to subside.

"He deserved it," she whispered to herself, trying to rationalize her actions.

Her mind in a fog, she walked over to the bedroom light and flicked it on.

Blood seeped through the bedsheets and was splattered across the walls.

Blood everywhere.

Susan shuddered with panic. There was no way in hell she could clean this mess up.

But she had to survive...And get away with the crime.

She began breaking things down, step by step. The first chore was to go into the shower and get cleaned up. She watched as Jeff's blood dripped off her and into the drain, her thoughts gathering.

Time to cover my ass, she thought, staring at her reflection in the fogged up bathroom mirror.

She then called Jeff's parents who lived over three hours away in Austin. Susan went into melodrama mode as the tears poured out.

"Susan?" Jeff's mother asked. "What is it?"

"It's Jeff," Susan said. "He came home from his boxing lessons and just went wacko."

"What do you mean?"

"He started hitting me," Susan sobbed. "Started hitting Bradley."

"Oh God, no. That's not Jeff."

"He wouldn't stop."

"Put Jeff on the phone."

"He's not here," Susan said. "He just ran out of the house. He's gone for good this time. I know it."

"What was he so angry about?"

"He's on drugs," Susan said. "Has been for a long, long time. Cocaine. Marijuana. Now he has no money and we're in debt because of it. He was just so frustrated all the time but tonight.... Tonight he just went wacko."

"Jeff doesn't do drugs."

"Yes," Susan nodded. "He can't help it. It's a secret."

Susan then remained on the phone with Jeff's parents for over an hour. They tried to console her as she detailed all of his abuses. Finally, she hung up and realized that she had to take care of his body.

But how?

After a few moments, she thought of the fountain out by the back porch. Jeff had left the job unfinished, as per usual, but the hole was pre-dug!

Her adrenaline still pumping, Susan went into the garage and retrieved a dolly that the couple used earlier to roll some new furniture into the house. She untied Jeff's body and plopped him onto the dolly, rolling him down the hall and dropping him face first in the shallow grave next to the back porch.

Another problem arose, however, as Jeff's body had begun to stiffen from the rigor mortis. She bent his legs and torso as much as she could to make him fit in the shallow hole. Then she began pouring the dirt over him.

It would be morning soon and she hurried back into the house. Susan mopped up the blood, starting from the patio, down the hallway and then to the bedroom itself. She rolled up the bloody bed sheets, gagging from the gruesome sight, then placed them into large Hefty bags.

Susan then pulled the mattress from the bed and dragged it into the backyard as she didn't know how to go about cleaning it just yet.

THE NEXT DAY

The children awoke early and Susan took them to daycare. She then drove to the hardware store and purchased a couple gallons of paint.

Arriving back at the house, Susan fought through fatigue and began to clean. She painted the walls and bleached out the blood on the carpet.

After a few hours, everything looked neat and tidy except for a bleach stain on the carpet.

Jeff's parents worried about their son. In the afternoon, they called Susan and asked if Jeff had come back home.

"He came by," Susan said. "Got his stuff and left."

"What do you mean 'got his stuff and left'?"

"He got some clothes," Susan paused, trying to get her story straight. "We started fighting again. He started yelling at me. Got a bottle of bleach and began pouring it around our bedroom. I thought he was going to set the place on fire."

"He wouldn't do that."

"He did," Susan said, adamant.

"We need to talk to him."

"He left his cell phone here," Susan said.

After the next few hours, Susan would field calls from Jeff's employer and a neighbor. She told Jeff's boss that he had gone "wacko" and told the neighbor the same story she had told Jeff's parents.

The neighbor advised Susan to call the police.

Susan realized that the noose around her neck would close fast if she didn't do something. She had to take the initiative somehow to get ahead of the investigation as Jeff's parents and the police would have plenty of questions.

First, she went to the emergency room and reported that she had been beaten by Jeff.

The doctor on duty at the time, Stephen Fischer, stated that he believed Susan and told her to report the injuries to the police. Later, under cross-examination, the prosecutor got Dr. Fischer to admit that he really didn't know how Susan got those injuries and was going strictly off what he told her.

On January 15th, 2003, two days after she had murdered Jeff, Susan entered Precinct Four of the Harris County Constable's office. She filed a report on Jeff, once again using the same story that she had told his parents and her neighbor.

She had physical evidence to back up her story as she had cuts on her hands and a bruise on her thigh.

"I'm scared of what will happen when he comes back," Susan informed the reporting officer. "He's abusive and violent."

A restraining order against Jeff was filed.

"She had a bruise on her thigh," Orange said. "The police chalked up her complaint as a routine domestic violence case."

A WEB OF DECEIT

Three days later, however, Susan felt the pressure of her lies. Jeff's parents kept calling, family and friends, plus his employer.

There was no way she could keep up this charade.

Looking out the window, she saw their dog, a chow mix, had dug up the area where Jeff had been buried. She could see the dog had unearthed Jeff's arm as well as the back of his head.

The chow had tried to pull its owner from its burial place, however, and in doing so had bitten off Jeff's hand.

The dog played with the hand as if it were a toy, laying it on the patio.

It was a sick irony, as Jeff would often beat the dog and once threw it against the wall.

But the visual of her husband's half-buried body and dismembered hand sent Susan into a panic.

She needed to tell someone.

Susan placed her daughter Kailey and son Bradley into her car and headed straight toward her mother's house.

She told her mother the same story as before, informing her about the restraining order.

"He'll kill me if he comes back," Susan said. Her voice was now half-hearted. She had to tell someone. If she was going to come clean, it would have to be with her mother first.

"Susan, you really need to tell me what's going on."

"It wasn't just a fight," Susan said to her mother, fighting back tears. "And he didn't just run away."

"What do you mean?"

"He's dead."

"You're overreacting."

"No," Susan said. " I stabbed him. I buried him in the backyard. I didn't know what else to do."

Susan slumped forward and put her head on the table, sobbing.

Her mother called Susan's sister Cindy to come pick up the children. She then had to save her daughter at all costs, calling up numerous defense attorneys to price them accordingly.

Her mother hired Neal Davis, who came to the home. He then informed the police of Jeff's body in the back yard.

The police searched the home and found evidence of blood that Susan had failed to clean during her bleach wash.

THE TRIAL

The case took over thirteen months to reach a trial which started on February 24th, 2004.

Susan would stake the stand and claim self-defense.

"Susan had a rough go of it in the trial," Orange said. "Every part of it was televised and she was going up against a prosecuting attorney named Kelly Siegler. Siegler was ferocious and often used out of the box methods to defeat defense attorneys."

Once the trial began, Siegler immediately pounced on Susan like Mike Tyson trying to finish his foe in the first few seconds of a fight.

The first question Siegler asked Susan was "Have you ever lied to avoid getting into trouble?"

"No," Susan said in an unsure voice "I can't say I ever have."

"Siegler's tactic was to show Susan to be the liar she was," Orange said. "Everyone on the jury has lied before. Show right off the bat, the prosecution hit a home run."

"He attacked me with a knife," Susan said. "He kept yelling 'Die, bitch! Die bitch!'"

"Why did you stab him almost 200 times?" the prosecutor asked.

"Once I started," Susan began to cry. "I couldn't stop. If I stopped, he would have killed me."

Siegler then called Susan's tears "fake." She argued that Susan killed Jeff in order to collect on a $200,000 life insurance policy.

Siegler then had the Wright's actual bed brought into the courtroom. The prosecutor asked a younger male member of her staff to lay on the bed while she re-enacted the murder for the jury. The man struggled against the restraints much like Jeff would have. Siegler then proceeded to "stab the victim" over and over again...197 times...stimulating Susan's act down to the very last stroke of the blade.

The jury was shaken by this visual. They would deliberate over five and a half-hours before declaring that Susan was guilty of murder.

"She stabbed Jeff at least 197 times," Orange said. "I say at least 197 times because the coroners determined that she stabbed him in numerous spots more than once. They couldn't determine the exact amount."

Susan's married life had echoed what she saw in her own childhood when she witnessed her mother go through nightly beat downs at the hands of her father. Susan's mother would later deny this but Susan's sister, Cindy, would confirm that their mother was indeed the victim of abuse. Cindy had a Ph.D., in psychology and would state that witnessing these beatings left a scar in Susan's memories that she could never erase.

"She stabbed Jeff for all the times that he punched her in the chest, and she stabbed him for all of the times that he raped her in the middle of the night. And she stabbed Jeff because he was just like her father."

In March of 2004, Susan would be sentenced to 25 years to left for killing Jeff Wright.

Things took a turn in her favor, however, when Misty McMichael came forward and relayed her experience with Jeff Wright. McMichael was another former stripper who had dated Jeff for four years and verified that she had been the victim of his violence and abuse.

The Fourteenth Court of Appeals of Texas then gave Susan a new hearing.

A video recording of Bradley was brought in as evidence for the new trial. Bradley was filmed in 2003 by Harris County Child Protective Services when he was four-years-old. In the video, Bradley was working on a coloring book.

"Have you ever seen your dad hit your mom?" the interviewer asked.

"No," Bradley said.

"Did you ever see bruises on your mom?"

"She has some on her legs."

"How did she get them?"

"I don't know."

The prosecution would later try to insinuate that Susan had drugged Jeff, noting the level of GHB (the 'date rape' drug) in her system. The toxicology report would reveal had Jeff had used cocaine but less than .1 gram was in his body. There was also 33 mg of GHB found but this is a naturally occurring chemical which exacerbates as the body decomposes. The toxicologist could only say there was a "fifty-fifty" chance that GHB was administered to Jeff during the night of his murder.

Kevin Conboy, one of Jeff's co-workers, would be called to testify at the re-sentencing trial. The prosecution wanted to reiterate the fact that Susan was overly concerned about Jeff's life insurance policy.

"It was clear that the conversation was about the insurance policy and whether or not Jeff had turned in the insurance policy," Conboy said. "That he would get it taken care of and he would turn in paperwork and he also said, 'If I die, you will be a very rich woman.'"

This go around, however, the defense team would make sure the jury knew about Susan's abuse. They would call on one of Jeff's brother-in-laws, Brian Roberts, who witnessed a fight between the couple.

"I saw her turn to Jeff with a knife," Roberts said.

He also claimed that he spoke to Susan about Jeff's abuse.

"I asked her if it had happened before."

"What was her answer?" the defense attorney asked.

"'Yes, 2,3,5 more than 6 times,' she said."

Kay Wright, Jeff's mother, would take the stand as well.

"He said, 'I love you, Mom'" Kay said, fighting back tears as she described her son's last words to her. She informed the jury that she had no reason to believe that Susan was lying when she said she kicked out Jeff during that fateful evening.

"I said, 'Has Jeff come back?' And she said, 'Yes he's come back.' And she said he got some of his clothes and he took my clothes and put bleach all over them in the bedroom and she also said he'd left a note that said thanks for betraying me or something like that. She said, 'If anything ever happens to me, I want my kids to live with my sister.' I said, 'Nothing is going to happen. Jeffrey will come home and we'll straighten this thing out."

Kay listened to all of this not knowing that her son Jeff lay dead, stabbed nearly 200 times just a few feet away from Susan.

But the defense had a better case this go around. The twenty-five-year punishment was reversed. Susan had been given leeway as she convinced the jury that she suffered from battered women syndrome.

"At the end of the day," Orange said. "This was an impulse murder. Susan had to tie Jeff down and most likely drug him up. Helpless and not knowing what else to do, she committed one of the most brutal murders I had ever studied. But she was not a psychopath. She was an abused woman who snapped and did something psychopathic. That doesn't mean that she shouldn't be duly punished. And it doesn't necessarily mean that she's a psychopath frothing at the mouth."

They would take off five years from Susan's sentence and make her eligible for parole.

"If we are to believe that Susan's allegations of abuse are true," Orange said. "Then she definitely was a poster child for battered women's syndrome. In other words, she could not leave Jeff whenever anyone looking at the situation objectively would. She acquired a learned state of helplessness. She lost hope at her ability to change the situation. There are some psychologists who believe that the battered woman can become homicidal when they are pushed to the brink. When Susan saw her son being hit by Jeff, she lost it."

Bradley and Kailey would later be adopted by Jeff's brother, Ronald.

HUSBAND KILLER : THE TRUE STORY OF AUDREY MARIE HILLEY

ANNA DELANEY

Audrey Marie Hilley

"That woman was pitiful," said Janice Hinds, 50, one of two neighbours who called police and cared for Hilley after spotting her sprawled on the deck of Thomason's home.

"We didn't know she was Marie Hilley. She didn't look like Marie Hilley," said Hinds, who grew up in the same Blue Mountain cotton-mill town as Hilley. "Marie Hilley was a sophisticated lady. She had pride in her looks, her dress."[1]

Her Early Life

Audrey Marie Hilley was born on June 4th, 1933 in Blue Mountain, Alabama. Her parents, Huey and Lucille Frazier, worked hard at the Linen Mill to provide for their family, and Marie (as she was known) was often looked after by relatives when her mother returned to work shortly after she was born.

Huey and Lucille loved their only child but showed their love with material things rather than affection and time. She was always well-dressed and had nice things, and as a result, Marie became rather spoilt. She was well known for her temper tantrums when things didn't go her way, and her parents, possibly out of guilt for not being there, rarely checked her for her behaviour.[2]

The Fraziers were proud people and were determined that their only child would not spend her life working in the same mills as they, and most of the town's inhabitants, had always done. They wanted more for their daughter and instilled in her an ambition to be a secretary, a lofty ambition for someone from a mill town.

In 1945, the Fraziers moved from Blue Mountain to Anniston, and Marie enrolled at Quintard Junior High School. Anniston was a whole new world to the girl who had felt she was above the rest in her old hometown. Marie went from being a big fish in a small pond to a small fish in a much more upscale lake, and for the first time in her life found herself at a disadvantage. In Anniston, all the girls wore nice dresses and what was more, some of their parents were the owners of the same mills that Marie's parents worked at.

Marie threw herself into her studies, making a name for herself as a diligent, intelligent student, and she integrated herself into new social circles – her friends were from privileged families and Marie wanted to be a part of that.

It wasn't just the teachers for whom Marie stood out, though. She was also a pretty girl and had her fair share of the attention from the boys, too. In fact, by the end of the 7th grade of Junior High School, Marie Hilley had been voted the prettiest girl in school by the yearbook staff.

It was around this time that 16-year-old Frank Hilley noticed 12-year-old Marie, and by the time he graduated High School, he was in love.[3]

Frank and Marie

In contrast to the Frazier family, who loved their daughter but showed no affection, Frank Hilley's family was warm and affectionate. The Hilleys worked in the other big industry of the area – pipe making - and even though they did not have much money, Clarence and Carrie Hilley made a happy, comfortable home for their three children – Frank, Jewel and Freeda.

Marie's parents did not approve of Frank – he was not from one of the affluent families of Anniston and Huey and Lucille wanted more for their daughter – but Marie was happy to be Frank's girl, and in return, he treated her like a princess.

Frank joined the Navy after finishing High School and was assigned to Guam but the distance between them bothered Frank. He was worried that with him so far away, and with so much time apart, Marie might find someone else so, on May 8th, 1951, before 17-year-old Marie had even finished High School, the young couple married.

Married Life

Marie remained in Anniston to finish her education and then joined Frank in Long Beach, California before the couple moved to Boston where Frank finished his stint in the Navy. It was while they were in Boston that they discovered Marie was pregnant with their first child, and the couple moved back to Anniston and bought a small home. Frank secured a job with a local foundry, and Marie found work as a secretary. Like all couples, the pair had their ups and downs, but for the most part, they seemed happy.

Their first child, Michael Hilley, was born on November 11th, 1952.

The Troubles Begin

Marie had been brought up to want the best of everything. While Frank was still in the Navy he had sent all of his paychecks home to his young wife, and yet when the time had come for her to join her new husband in California she had no money to pay for the journey. She had been spending his wages without telling him, and his parents had had to finance Marie's travel in order for her to join her new husband.

Despite the extra financial burdens having a young baby places on a family, Marie's spending didn't decrease. She wanted nice clothes and expensive home furnishings, and Frank, not liking to upset his wife, gave in to her, just as her parents had when she was a girl. Marie was a woman who was used to getting her own way.[4]

In 1959 Marie's behaviour began to become more sinister. She started taunting Frank, waving love letters she said were from other men in front of him but not letting him read them. She would then leave the torn up pieces where her husband could find them. Frank pieced them together, and it became clear that his wife had written them herself. When he confronted her she said she was afraid he didn't love her anymore and wanted to make him jealous.

By this time, Marie was spending double her take-home pay from her own job on fine clothes and luxuries. To prevent Frank, who was extremely responsible financially, from finding out she would get up early in the morning to check the mail and hide the bills.

Marie became pregnant again, and on January 14th, 1960 she gave birth to a baby daughter, whom they named Carol Marie.[5]

Carol

By the time Carol was born, things should have been looking up for the family. Frank had been promoted at work, and Marie had developed a reputation as a first class executive secretary. However, as the family's income rose, so did Marie's spending. Furthermore, she was becoming known for a peculiar situation at work. While her bosses loved her for her politeness and diligence, her co-workers greatly disliked her. They found her to be very judgemental of those around her and felt that she put on airs and graces and acted as if her co-workers were 'beneath' her. When she became disliked she would leave, and complain to friends and family that her colleagues had 'ganged up' on her and driven her from her job. Her employers, though, always gave her exemplary references, and she never found it difficult to get another job. In fact, Marie Hilley worked for some of the most powerful and affluent men in Anniston.[6]

Marie was disappointed with her daughter, Carol. She wanted her daughter to wear pretty dresses and have bows in her hair, while Carol was more of a tomboy and would often go to football games with her father. The pair developed a close father/daughter relationship and Marie was deeply resentful and jealous. She lamented the fact that her daughter was not feminine and demure and the pair argued constantly. Marie was much closer to her son, Mike, and like her parents before her never dished out discipline. Materially, the children wanted for nothing. Emotionally, it was a different story.

Going Up in the World

In 1962, Marie instigated a move to McClellan Boulevard, which was much closer to the houses of the affluent residents of Anniston that she so desperately tried to emulate. She felt that they were 'her' people. That same year, Marie's parents – Huey and Lucille moved in with the Hilleys.[7]

Marie's behaviour was becoming more and more out of control, and Frank was becoming increasingly concerned. He would often sit up with her during the night as she shook violently, unable to calm her. Perhaps the financial hole she had dug for the family was beginning to take its toll on Marie's psyche – by this time she had opened a Post Office Box and was having some of her bills sent there in order to avoid detection by Frank.

When the money ran out Marie started taking out loans. Frank was a well-respected man in the area and loans were secured against his good name and standing in the community. But creditors became concerned when bills and loan payment dates came and went without being settled, as Frank had always been a man who paid on time.[8]

On December 11th, 1965, Marie's father, Huey, died of cancer at the age of 57.[9]

In 1972, Mike graduated from High School and decided to pursue a career in the ministry, for which he went away to college.

Marie's behaviour towards her daughter, Carol, became more extreme. She often accused her of being a lesbian and would rant at Carol's female friends. Her paranoia at being found out in the lies regarding money must have been affecting her, because she also, around this time, stopped Frank from talking to his friends on the 'phone. It was also around this period of time that Frank Hilley became sick.[10]

Frank

During 1974 Frank had long periods of sickness. He put his frequent illnesses down to something he'd eaten, but soon the fatigue, vomiting and nausea could not be explained away by food. One day Frank came home from work early after succumbing to yet another bout of sickness, to find his wife in bed with her boss. His wife's spending suddenly made sense – she was sleeping with her employers for money. Frank was disgusted with his wife's behaviour but felt too ill and weak to deal with it. Instead, he turned to his son, Mike, who was by this time an ordained minister.[11]

However, that phone call, in which Frank arranged to meet Mike in Georgia where he now lived, was overheard by Audrey, who was listening in on an extension. From that moment on, Frank's symptoms worsened considerably, and he became seriously ill.[12]

On May 19th, 1975 Frank couldn't stand it any longer, and he consulted Dr Earl Jones, who diagnosed him initially with a viral stomach ache.[13] Dr Earl prescribed various medications, but nothing seemed to be helping. Frank's sister Freeda came to visit him, and he told her that he feared he was going to die, as he had never been so sick. He also told her that Marie had been administering him medicine via a syringe on the Dr's orders.[14]

On May 23rd, 1975, Frank was admitted to the Regional Medical Center. Tests indicated liver failure, and subsequently infectious hepatitis.[15] Frank was desperately ill, jaundiced and hallucinating. Mike, who had travelled to be with his father, had to restrain Frank from jumping out of the window. In the early hours of May 25th, Mike left the hospital to pick up his Grandmothers so that they could see Frank, but when he returned his mother was asleep and his father was dead. Frank Hilley was 45.[16]

Because of Frank's sudden death, an autopsy was performed, with Marie's blessing. Tests showed that Frank did indeed have hepatitis, along with swelling of the lungs and kidneys, inflammation of the stomach, and bilateral pneumonia.[17]

Life After Frank

With Frank's death being confirmed as being of natural causes, Marie made a claim on his life insurance and received a payment of

$31,140.[18] Marie went on a spending spree, indulging her love of luxury items. She bought new clothes, jewelery, and a new car. Her mother, Lucille, was still living with Marie and Carol and received a diamond ring. Carol herself was treated to numerous gifts, including a car and a stereo. It was hardly the behaviour of a grieving widow.[19]

In 1976 Mike and his then wife Teri moved in with the family. Shortly after Frank's death, Lucille had been diagnosed with cancer. Her health was failing and they were happy to help. However, it wasn't a good move for the young couple. Marie was restless, and often complained to anyone who would listen that nobody loved her, and would frequently complain about her boss and her job. She was highly dissatisfied with her life, and to make matters worse Marie and Carol fought endlessly, making family life fraught. Mike would often find himself torn between his mother, who would constantly demand his attention, and his wife, Teri, who had begun experiencing ill health since moving in with Marie. Hospitalised four times with illness, Teri also suffered a miscarriage, and the young couple decided to move out.

They found an apartment and were ready to move in, but the night before their move Marie's house caught fire. Mike and Teri moved into their apartment, with Marie, Carol and Lucille in tow. Repairs were soon made to Marie's house, but the night before his mother was due to go home, Mike's neighbour's apartment suffered the same fate and went up in flames. Mike and Teri had no choice but to move back in with Marie, Carol and Lucille. They were back where they began.[20]

A Strange Series of Events

Mike and Teri finally found their own home and moved away from Marie. On January 4th, 1977, Lucille lost her battle against widespread, aggressive cancer. Marie again came into money – a small sum of $600 from a burial policy.

Marie became well known to the local police. She was constantly reporting strange occurrences at her home. As well as petty thefts, she claimed that a fire had been started in her closet late one night. Coincidentally, Marie's neighbour, Doris Ford reported an almost identical fire in her own house (to which Marie had a key) the same night. There followed a succession of reports by both women of nuisance phone calls and other grievances.

Marie came up with many theories about where the harassment of both herself and her neighbour was coming from. She told Detective Gary Caroll that she suspected someone at the phone company of making the calls, as the calls seemed only to happen when the trace was taken off of her phone. She also claimed that one of her former employers had tried to force her to have sex and was harassing her because of her refusal. Yet another theory put forward by Marie was that, shortly after Frank's death, two men had arrived at her house demanding repayment of gambling debts.

When police put a trace on Doris Ford's phone, however, the calls were traced back to the Jenkins Manufacturing Plant, which just so happened to be where Marie was working.[21]

In 1978, Marie and Carol moved to Florida to live with Mike and Teri. Carol had just graduated, and Marie found herself a job in an office. Her out of control spending habits continued to cause problems when she ran up over $600 on Mike's credit card, promising to pay him back. This living arrangement only lasted a few short months, however, before Marie and Carol returned to Anniston.[22]

Mike and Teri were happy to see Marie leave. By that time they had a baby son called Joshua, and Mike feared that Marie would take the baby and disappear as she seemed to have an unhealthy fixation on him.[23]

Carol's Turn

Marie had no home of her own to return to when she and Carol moved back to Anniston. At first, they stayed with Freeda, Frank's sister, and then they moved in with Carrie Hilley, Frank's mother.

Once they were settled at Carrie's house, the strange happenings recommenced. Items went missing, phone lines were cut, and small fires were started. Illness also struck the household – Carrie Hilley started suffering from nausea and vomiting.

Marie started a new job, and very quickly started an affair with her boss, Harold Dillard, and began manipulating him to leave his wife. At the same time, she also started seeing Calvin Robertson, an old school friend. Calvin believed Marie when she told him she had cancer and needed expensive treatment, and he gladly gave her the money for the 'fictitious' illness. When Marie told him some time later that she was now cancer-free he was elated, and so smitten that he would have done anything for her.

It was also during this time that Marie began buying insurance policies. Not only did she take out fire insurance, cancer insurance, and her own life insurance, she also took out insurance policies on the lives of her two children. Mike was insured for $25,000 while Carol had two policies on her life, totalling $39,000.

Carol's senior prom came in April 1979. During the evening Carol started to feel ill. It wasn't enough to make her leave the party, though, so she ignored her symptoms. The next day, however, she was so ill during a church service that she had to leave the service early and vomited in the car park. Coincidentally, Carrie Hilley had also taken ill at church and was taken to hospital after fainting.[24]

By August 1979 Carol had been admitted to the Emergency Room several times with nausea and vomiting. After yet another episode of sickness in August, Marie gave her daughter an injection into her hip, which she said would ease the nausea. Instead of easing, however, Carol's illness took a serious downturn. Not only did the injection not ease Carol's sickness, it also caused her fingers and legs to become numb and weak.

On August 22nd, 1979 she was admitted to the Anniston Hospital by Dr Warren Sarrell. When, by August 29th Dr Sarrell had been unable to find a cause for Carol's symptoms, he sent her for a psychiatric evaluation at the Carraway Methodist Hospital in Birmingham. While under the care of Dr John Elmore, Carol was given two further injections by her mother – injections which, she was told, would help with her weak legs. She told Carol that the injections had been supplied by Doris Ford, who was a registered nurse, and that Carol could tell no-one as Doris would get into trouble if she was found out.

On September 18th, 1979, with Carol still in the hospital, Marie asked Dr Elmore what was wrong with her daughter. He told her that she was suffering from vitamin deficiencies and malnutrition, and, in his opinion, lead poisoning. Carol took exception to this diagnosis and, against Dr Elmore's advice, discharged Carol from the hospital.

On September 19th, Carol was once again admitted to the hospital, this time to the University of Alabama Hospital in Birmingham. The same day, Marie was arrested as her fraudulent ways finally caught up with her. Her arrest was what, ultimately, saved Carol's life. Marie was taken in for questioning, and Carol was examined by Dr Brian Thompson, who noticed that, along with the numbness in her hands and feet, Carol also had striations on her nails, called Aldridge Mee's Lines. He explained that these markings were typical of arsenic poisoning, and ordered tests on Carol's hair.

The initial findings revealed that Carol had over 50 times the normal arsenic level of human hair. Shockingly, when more detailed tests were carried out on October 3rd, 1979 they showed that the hair close to Carol's scalp had over 100 times the normal levels, while hair further down the hair shaft the levels were lower, right down to zero at the ends. This indicated, according to Forensic Scientist John Case, that Carol had been systematically poisoned with arsenic over a period of four to eight months, with the dosages given in increasingly higher strengths.

Furthermore, with Marie unable to be with her daughter, Carol's conditioned improved dramatically during her time at the hospital.[25]

On the strength of these findings, Frank Hilley's body was exhumed, and once again large levels of arsenic were found. His cause of death was changed to that of arsenic poisoning. The same substance was also discovered to have been present in both Lucille Frazier and Carrie Hilley (who had died recently) at the time of their deaths, although not fatal amounts.[26]

On October 9th, 1979, while still incarcerated for the fraudulent charges, Marie Hilley was arrested for the attempted murder of Carol. As part of their ongoing, and increasingly serious, investigations the Anniston police found a vial in Marie's purse – a vial which testing confirmed contained arsenic.

On November 9th, 1979, Marie made bail and was released, under the name of Emily Stephens, to a local motel. However, Marie was not going to just sit and await her trial, and somewhere between October 9th and October 18th, Marie disappeared. A note was found in her motel room, suggesting that she 'might' have been kidnapped.

Audrey Marie Hilley was now a fugitive and would remain so for more than three years.[27]

A New Identity

There were only a few clues for the police to go on after Marie disappeared. Margaret Key, Marie's Aunt, reported that her home had been broken into and that her car and some clothes had disappeared. The police called in the FBI, but once the car was found abandoned in Georgia the trail went cold very quickly.

On January 11th, 1980, Marie Hilley, still a fugitive, was indicted for the murder of her husband, Frank Hilley.

Marie, meanwhile, had assumed a new identity in Florida. Robbi Hannon, as she was now known, was working her charm on a man called John Homan. Robbi told John tales of her imaginary tragic past, and John, who hadn't had the easiest of lives himself, fell for both the stories and for Robbi. She told him that she had lost her children in a car accident and John felt as though he had found a kindred spirit.

He fell in love, hook, line, and sinker.

On May 29th, 1981 Robbi and John were married, after which they moved to Marlow, New Hampshire. They both found work there and rented a house. Robbi's new job was in customer service at the Central Screw Corporation, where she excelled. The men found her to be fun, while her co-workers, for the most part, found her pleasant, although a few took a dislike to her. She regaled the staff with stories of a wealthy family in Texas, whose fortune she would inherit one day, and garnered sympathy by telling them about her two children dying in a car accident.

She would also talk of an identical twin sister called Teri Martin, who lived in Texas, making frequent reference to her.

Robbi would, from time to time, complain of searing headaches, and told John that she was seeking treatment from specialists. Until one day, Robbi came to John and told him it had been discovered that she was suffering from an incurable blood disease. It was her twin sister, Teri, who would be looking after Robbi when she made one last trip to Texas in search of a cure, and in September 1982, Robbi left Marlow to seek treatment.

Of course, there was no incurable disease, and no twin sister, either. Robbi only stayed in Texas for a few days, and then made her way to Florida, where she bleached her hair blond, and found work as a secretary, using the name Teri Martin. During her six weeks at her new job, Teri confided in her boss, Jack McKenzie, about her terminally ill twin sister Robbie. In early November, Teri called Jack and told him Robbi had died, and that she was needed in New Hampshire.

On November 10th, 'Teri' called John Homan and told him his wife had died, and the following day she flew back to New Hampshire.

During her time away, 'Teri' had lost a lot of weight, and changed her hair color to blond, so John easily accepted that this was his dead wife's twin sister. The pair went to the local paper and placed an obituary for Robbi, and then John took Teri to his wife's workplace – The Central Screw Corporation – and introduced the workers to Robbi's twin sister. While some of the staff accepted Teri's appearance, some did not and were highly suspicious.

Teri insisted on moving in with John Homan, saying they needed to help each other grieve, and she found herself a job as a secretary at a book printing company.

Meanwhile, the suspicions were still rising at Robbi's old workplace, and a few of the doubters decided to take a closer look into Robbi's obituary. Their suspicions were confirmed when they discovered that the details mentioned in the paper were fictitious, and they took those suspicions to the police.

Arrested

On January 12th, 1983, the police apprehended Teri at work. They had been watching her and thought she might be another fugitive, Terry Lynn Clifton. However, when they asked her her name she told them it was Audrey Marie Hilley, and that she was wanted for fraud. The local police ran a check on her name and discovered that she was wanted for much more than bad checks.

On January 19th, 1983, Marie was brought back to Anniston. Carol was desperate to see her mother, to find some answers, but although Marie professed her love for her daughter she gave no explanation for the poisoning. Prosecutors were worried that Carol's love for her mother would go in Marie's favour and that Carol would not say anything against her mother.

They needn't have worried.

Carol's testimony about her mother giving her the injections was solid. Marie had told her attorneys that after her arrest in 1979 she had been interviewed but she failed to mention that that interview had been recorded. During that interview, Marie admitted to giving Carol the injections and the recording was there for all to hear. Carol's defense fell apart.

The jury needed only three hours to return their verdicts – guilty of the murder of Frank Hilley, and of the attempted murder of Carol Hilley.

Judge Sam Monk sentenced Marie to life imprisonment for Frank's murder, plus twenty years for the poisonings, and on June 9th, 1983, Marie was taken to Tutwiler State Women's Prison in Wetumpka, Alabama.

Marie's Escape

Marie was a perfect prisoner. She never caused trouble and was classified as a minimum security prisoner. This classification meant that she was eligible for leave from the prison. Between late 1986 and February 1987, Marie had left prison for eight hours on four occasions, returning on time with each leave.

On February 19th, 1987, Marie left the prison on a three-day leave pass. John had, by this time, moved to Anniston so that he and his wife could spend her leave together whenever they could.

On February 22nd, Marie arranged to meet John at her parents' graves. Marie never showed up, and John found, instead, a note from his wife.

"I hope you will be able to forgive me," it read. *"I'm getting ready to leave. It will be best for everybody. We'll be together again. Please give me an hour to get out of town."*

John took the note to the police, and, given Marie's past cunning, they assumed she was already far out of state, and started, once again, searching for her.[28]

Her Death

Marie hadn't gone far. On February 26th, 1987, Aniston police received a phone call. Marie had been found huddled behind a house, apparently having wandered in the woods for four days. The weather had been terrible – heavy rain and low temperatures – and Marie was suffering from hypothermia and delirium. Marie started having convulsions, and, in the ambulance on the way to the hospital, Audrey Marie Hilley took her last breath.

On February 28th, 1987, Marie was buried next to her husband, Frank, at their children's request.[29] Her second husband, John Homan, died two years later in 1989 while working as a caretaker in Anniston. He intervened in a fight and was stabbed to death. Marie's note to John, in which she said that they would be together again, had come true a lot sooner than anyone would have predicted.[30]

TRACEY GRISSOM

Claiming to be a victim of rape and other abuses, a distraught Tracey Grissom would travel to her ex-husband Hunter's workplace and shoot him six times in the back, receiving a twenty-five-year life sentence for his murder.

Her defense attorney would argue that Tracey was motivated by post-traumatic stress disorder caused by her Hunter's constant abuse and sexual assaults. One jury member had even asked the judge to be lenient in her sentencing as they were not allowed to hear details of her Hunter's alleged abuses (beatings, rape, sodomy).

But what really happened in the years that led up to May 15th, 2012? Was she in fact the victim of years of abuse by a psychotic husband? Or did she want to cash in on his $100,000 life insurance policy?

INSTANT ATTRACTION

The couple would meet during a dinner party in 2003 in Tuscaloosa, Alabama. Tracey was twenty-one years old and going through a divorce. She had a son, James Michael, from the previous marriage.

Family and friends would describe the union as "love at first sight." Hunter was blown away by the young Tracey's blue eyes and facial beauty.

"For him, it was love at first sight," crime author William Phelps said. "She was gorgeous."

A whirlwind courtship would ensue and the couple would elope in 2004.

"In the beginning, it was good," Tracey told CBS' 48 hours. "We had a friendship. Just your normal, honeymoon phase marriage."

"He was fun," Tracey said. "And he was attractive."

Hunter was two years younger than Tracey, however, and his mother felt that he had jumped the gun too early in the relationship.

Her words proved to be prophetic as after only eight months into the marriage, the marriage went south.

According to Tracey, their marital problems began with Hunter's drug addiction.

"I had caught him smoking marijuana," Tracey said. "Doing illegal things could cause a problem and I couldn't risk losing my son over."

Tracey claimed that she threatened her new spouse with a divorce but Hunter gave her his word that he would stop with his drug use. She stated that the relationship improved and the decided to start a construction company together.

"I took out an equity line to start a company," Tracey said. "Which was Grissom Construction. It was all in my name."

Hunter specialized in building elaborate boat docks. He had an artistic eye and could do docks, stairs, and other accouterments. The business began to grow in short order.

"They're going to take on the world," Phelps said. "They're going to be entrepreneurs and they're gonna make it."

They then had a daughter of their own, Anna Grace. The child was a long time coming for the couple. They had been trying for a long time as Tracey had five miscarriages before Anna Grace was born.

"She was premature," Tracey recalled. "Her heart and lungs were not developed. A very stressful time."

Behind closed doors things were rocky. On the surface, however, things looked good. They had a young family and were making money.

"All-American family," Phelps said. "White-picket fence. The whole nine yards. Middle-class. Suburbia. Maybe the Prince Charming that she's been waiting for."

But again, this was only on the surface. Tracey harbored secrets of her own. One of which was her own addiction to prescription drugs.

"Psychologically, there's something going on here," Phelps said. "There's something going on behind those beautiful eyes and it ain't good."

Tracey would often turn on on the children, showing off her temper. Then she would turn on Hunter.

"This would cause friction in the marriage," Phelps said. "And where there's friction, there's fire."

SETTING THE STAGE

Tracey would later state that Hunter would "act strangely" shortly before she filed divorce. She was a registered nurse and gave him an over-the-counter drug test. According to her, Hunter tested posted for marijuana, Oxycontin, opiates, and methamphetamine.

Hunter would later be arrested for marijuana possession but his family would insist that he never did the harder drugs.

Tracey would file for divorce in the summer of 2010 after six years of marriage. According to her, this would prompt physical abuse from Hunter.

Hunter had to move out but their divorce agreement would allow him access to the home.

"In September of 2010," Tracey recalled. "That was the first time he physically hit me. It (the abuse) got progressively worse. He had made the comments that if I told anybody he would kill me. I believed him."

Hunter' co-workers and family members would have a different take on the situation, however. His co-workers remembered a time when she tracked him down at one of the jobs and made a scene.

"She's screaming, jumping on him," Hunter's co-worker said. "Said something about him having another girlfriend and used the expression about, 'You are mine. I'll kill you. I'll kill you. You are mine."

"She's borderline demonic," Hunter's mother said. " mean, I absolutely believe—that she is that troubled."

Hunter's family continued to believe that he did not abuse Tracey.

"He did not have an abusive, an angry bone in his body," Hunter's aunt Gina said. "In fact, we kind of laughed at him because he was too laid-back."

The divorce was finalized in October of 2010.

EVIDENCE OF ABUSE?

Loran Richards was the first of Tracey's friends to notice the minor injuries on her body. She would inquire about the bruises but the answers she received were always evasive. Seeing Tracey with a black eye, however, forced her to try and get more answers.

"I said, Tracey, you may have terrible luck," Richards recalled. "But nobody is so unlucky that they trip, fall down the stairs, and hit their face on a baseball in the eye socket. So don't give me a lame excuse. You don't have to give me any excuse, but let's take a picture."

Tracey broke down. She gave her friend all of the grisly details, detailing the abuse she suffered at the hands of Hunter. Loran then became her advocate, taking pictures of Tracey's injuries. She would later state that she saw blood stains and other signs of abuse at Tracey's home.

THAT FATEFUL NIGHT

Now divorced, Hunter would arrive at Tracey's home on November 22nd, 2010.

According to Tracey, he then became enraged when Tracey told him that she had spent the night with a new lover.

"He told me that he was gonna kill me," Tracey recalled. Tracey stated that she tried to escape, running into the closet in order to "get away from the kids and to pray." Tracey's eleven-year-old son from a previous relationship was in the home as was the four-year-old daughter they have together.

Hunter caught up with her and knocked her to the ground. He tied a belt around her ankles and then began choking her.

Half-conscious, Tracey alleged to have been raped and sodomized.

The brutal attack would leave Tracey unconscious. She would wake up the next morning on the bathroom floor.

"I called Hunter," Tracey recalled. "I told him that I was bleeding and that I was hurt and that I needed help. And he told me, 'Fuck you. I hope you die."

Tracey wound up in the emergency room after the attack. Hospital records would show that she had a laceration on her head, bruises, and ligature marks on her feet.

Tracey would then be referred to the Turning Point domestic violence center.

Marian Waters would describe Tracey's injuries as among the worst she had ever seen in a twenty-year career.

Waters would testify that Tracey had suffered a horrific assault. She described her mental state as typical of someone who had just been raped; fearful, jumpy, fearing for her life.

Tracey had suffered a hematoma on her side that was the side of a grapefruit. She also claimed to have experienced rectal nerve damage which would require surgery as well as torn vaginal muscles requiring her to have a hysterectomy.

Police were called and Hunter would be arrested for rape, sodomy, kidnapping and domestic violence.

"And at that point, I feared for my life," Tracey recalled. "And I feared for my children's life."

A HIDDEN AGENDA

Hunter would be freed on bail but Tracey got a restraining order against him. She bought a gun and did not go anywhere unarmed.

She took photos of her injuries on the night of the alleged attack and texted them to Loran. Later, they would take more pictures.

Angered, Hunter would stop paying her spousal and child support. Tracey, however, may have had another scenario in mind for obtaining money.

She had forced Hunter to take out a $103,000 life insurance policy around the time their daughter was born.

On May 24, 2012, the day before Tracey shot Hunter, she would place a call to MetLife that was recorded.

"Thank you for calling MetLife, this is Pam. May I please have your name?"

"Tracey Grissom."

Tracey would then explain that she was angry that her husband stopped making payments on his policy. During their divorce proceedings, he had agreed to continue paying the premiums. Tracey stated she was calling to make sure that they had the correct address on file.

"Is there anything else I can do for you today?

"That's gonna be it!" Tracey said, hanging up.

"Well, May 14th was just like any other day," Tracey said, explaining the call to the insurance company. "However, I had moved four different times. Me and my children were running. We were running from Hunter. So I had called the company to let them know that they had my old address and to make an address change."

FALSE RAPE?

Shelly Standridge was hired by Hunter to defend him in the rape case. She would state that Hunter denied raping or even assaulting Tracey that night. Hunter did, however, admit to the fact that he and his wife had consensual sex that night...Rough consensual sex.

"So that night," Standridge said. "Hunter said that she was depressed and claiming she was going to kill herself. She was saying she wanted their relationship to work."

So she undressed in front of him. Her beauty was always impossible for Hunter to resist.

The two had sex despite Hunter having a new girlfriend at home.

Hunter's aunt, Gina, believed that Tracey wanted to kill Hunter before the rape case went to court.

"He had a new girlfriend, he was living with her," Phelps said. "He was moving on with his life. Hunter would claim that Tracey was jealous, obsessive, even stalked them."

"Hunter had moved on," Hunter's aunt said. "There was some court dates coming up that would prove that Hunter was innocent. There were court dates coming up that he would get visitation to his daughter. She had a lot to lose."

Tracey was on the anti-anxiety drug Klonopin. Hunter would tell his attorney that Tracey would take more than her prescribed dose. Because of this, she fell and cut her head. Hunter would then leave the house around 10:30 pm and go to his father's house. Tracey would call him hours later, at 3:20 am.

Hunter would state that Tracey had called to threaten him. She told him if he didn't want the responsibility of the children then she would make it where he would never be able to see them again.

Hunter's attorney did not know what Tracey's motive was for crying rape. She was very upset that he had a girlfriend.

MORE LIES...

Hunter would be arrested nearly twelve hours later, to his total shock.

Tracey would give her side of the story to the police which later is proven to be false.

She would tell police that Hunter had thrown her against the bathtub around 10 pm and claim to be unconscious until 4 am the next morning.

"But her phone records show she was on the phone all night, so she was never unconscious," Standridge said. "She was also using her data at 10:42 that night. She was using it again at 10:50 that night. ... She sends a text to her boyfriend at 1:49 am. She sends a text to her friend at 2:07 am. She sends another text to her boyfriend at 2:07 am."

Tracey would blame the calls on Hunter.

"All I do know is I was not the only person using my phone that night," Tracey said, suggesting that Hunter used her phone.

Medical records would show that Tracey's head wound was "purely superficial".

Only one suture was needed.

Furthermore, there was nothing on the medical record to support the fact that Tracey experienced vaginal and rectal tears. She did have bruises on her ankle and legs but the photos taken by police at the emergency room would not resemble the same photos that Tracey and her friend Loran would take days later. In the photos taken at the emergency room, an area of Tracey's body has no bruises. Days later, there is discoloration.

Tracey's attorney would blame the discrepancy on "blood thinners" which would cause Tracey to bruise easily.

There was also a discrepancy in her phone records. She would take a photo of her inner thigh, a deep bruise. This area of her body was not photographed by police during her emergency room visit. But on December 9th, almost two weeks later, Tracey took a photo of her inner thigh with the deep bruise

"He (Hunter) told me that he would make it to where nobody would ever want me," Tracey said after a 2010 attack. "I didn't report it because I thought he would kill me."

THE FINAL STRAW

Tracey woke up pissed on May 15th, 2012.

Hunter had been ordered to pay $2,100 a month for the rest of his life. He was not complying with the court order claiming that he was "out of work."

Tracey stated that she was on her way to a job interview when she saw a Grissom Construction sign out of the corner of her eye.

She stated that her initial plan was to take a photograph of Hunter at the job site in order to show proof that he was working as part of her litigation.

"I was getting ready to take the picture and when I looked up he was standing almost directly towards the front of the boat trailer," Tracey said. "He was looking back directly at me. He had this face, that's like mean - just, I don't know how to describe it. I mean, I see it over and over like it's right there all the time. He flipped me the bird, which to me was kinda like, 'Yeah I'm workin. Screw you.' And at that point, I panicked. At that point, I didn't know what else to do except to defend myself."

Tracey started firing. The first shot hit Hunter in the arm. He started to run and she fired again repeatedly. One of the bullets punctured Hunter's heart and he died of massive internal bleeding.

William Dockery was working with Hunter and was an eyewitness to the shooting. Hunter had turned to Dockery before the shooting and told him to "call the law". Before Dockery could pick up his cell phone, Tracey had commenced shooting.

Tracey then pulled out her own cell phone and called the cops on herself. She tearfully described that she had just murdered her husband.

CONFESSION

Tracey told detectives exactly what was going through her mind when she came upon Hunter at the construction site.

"Tell me about what happened," the detective said. "What led up to...what's going on."

"In November of 2010, he beat me unconscious and raped me...and, and left me for dead....and, and I finally pressed charges against him and he told me that he would make my life a living hell...and that's what he's done."

"What, what happened this morning that led up to you going..."

"I was going to work and I saw him...and he's been claiming that he-he's not working. And, so I pulled in there to take a picture of him...cause it was the truck that's still in my name...and the boat that's still in my name...and the trailer that's still in my name...He just stared at me and flipped me off...and I just went in there and shot him...I just shot him, I shot him, and I shot him."

Tracey would be distraught and tearful during her interrogation room confession. A few weeks later, however, she would call the insurance company to let them know that Hunter had died.

"Well, I was actually calling because I didn't know what I needed to do ... Hunter passed away May 15th and I actually am going a court case right now because it was due to self-defense..."

Hunter's family went ballistic over this. Tracey would claim that she had no money but she continued to pay his life insurance premiums.

"Even through the times when she's screamin' that she's destitute and has no money ... she continued to pay life insurance premium," Hunter's mother said.

"I don't think my sister concocted a story," Tracey's sister said. "Just so she could get insurance money. ... But that's all they (the prosecution) had."

THE TRIAL

Tracey's allegations of rape and sodomy would not be allowed in court testimony. She was allowed, however, to detail the effects of Hunter's abuse on her were.

Taking the stand, Tracey would lift up her shirt in court and show herself wearing a colostomy bag. She stated that she had undergone several surgeries after her husband's daily rapes wherein she suffered permanent rectal and vaginal damage.

Hunter's family was then allowed to speak at the hearing.

"This tremendous loss has changed me," Hunter's mother, Melanie Garner said. "And I don't know how to change back."

Chloe, Hunter's sister, had a victim's services officer read her letter in court.

"Tracey is psychotic," Chloe wrote. "She is the most selfish person human being on this earth."

"Every mother should pray every night that your son doesn't fall in love with someone like Tracey," Hunter's aunt, Gina Grissom said. "There have been lots of allegations against Hunter. We've never believed anything that has come out of her (Tracey's) mouth."

His aunt then looked directly at Tracey.

"Hunter was proud of his name. Why would you still choose to use our name, and bring it down?" suggesting that if Tracey hated him so much why didn't she go revert to her maiden name after the divorce.

The jurors would find Tracey guilty of murder. She would be sentenced to twenty-five years in prison.

One of the jurors, Janice Kelly, would contact Grissom's attorney Warren Freeman the morning after the trial. She had remorse over her decision and said that she wouldn't have convicted her had they had the rapes and abuse allegations been introduced as evidence.

"I feel I made a mistake," Kelly said. "If I had to do it over again, we'd have had a hung jury. We didn't get her side. She did not get a fair trial."

"We voted to convict because there was no dispute that Tracey shot Hunter," the jury foreman wrote in a letter that was addressed in the courthouse. "Jurors didn't believe prosecutor claims that she did it in order to collect a life insurance policy. We felt the shooting was a crime of passion, not for financial gain and that she should be sentenced accordingly. I wish we had seen evidence of the rape allegation. We feel that she just 'lost it.'"

"It's not fair, it's not fair!" Tracey sobbed as she was led out of the courthouse and to jail.

"We think the sentencing was too harsh," Tracey's attorney Warren Freeman said. "Considering you have the foreperson of the jury actually saying, we don't feel like she should be punished according to being found guilty of murder. Let's just say that there will be a basis for a new trial, and part of it will be something that the jurors saw that they weren't supposed to see and I'm going to just leave it at that until I file my motion."

"My son died running for his life," Hunter's mother said. "I don't know what was running through his mind but I hear him say 'momma.'"

"People who think that I murdered him in cold blood," Tracey said. "Either don't know the whole story or don't know everything that's happened.

Tracey was asked on CBS' 48 hours if she regretted pulling the trigger on that fateful day.

"No," she said flatly. "Because if I hadn't I would be dead. I truly believe that."

"She has a way of making everything she does look right," Hunter's aunt, Gina scoffed.